The Scholastic **BIG** Book of
Holidays
Around the Year

by Susan Dillon

A must-have classroom collection!

NEW YORK ★ TORONTO ★ LONDON ★ AUCKLAND ★ SYDNEY

MEXICO CITY ★ NEW DELHI ★ HONG KONG ★ BUENOS AIRES

■SCHOLASTIC
Teaching
Resources

~ Dedication ~

I'd like to dedicate this book. . .
to Karen Baicker for giving a friend an invaluable contact;
to Sarah Longhi for molding me into a book writer;
to my husband, family, and friends for encouraging me constantly;
and to my children for making every day a holiday.

Credits

"La Thunka" (page 16). From *Celebrations Around the World: A Multicultural Handbook* by Carole S. Angell. Copyright © 1996 by Carole S. Angell. Reprinted by permission of Fulcrum Publishing Co.

"Columbus Sing-Along" (page 41) and "100th Day of School" (page 66). From *50 Thematic Songs Sung to Your Favorite Tunes* by Meish Goldish. Copyright (c) 1999 by Meish Goldish. Reprinted by permission of Scholastic Inc.

"I, Too, Sing America" (page 61). From *The Collected Poems of Langston Hughes* by Langston Hughes. Copyright © 1994 by The Estate of Langston Hughes. Used by permission of Alfred A. Knopf, a division of Random House, Inc.

"Rain Forest" (page 93). From *101 Science Poems and Songs for Young Learners* by Meish Goldish. Copyright © 1996 by Meish Goldish. Reprinted by permission of Scholastic Inc.

Edited by Sarah Glasscock
Cover art by Dave Clegg
Cover design by Gerard Fuchs
Interior illustrations by Milk & Cookies
Illustrations pages 37 and 44 by Anne Kennedy;
page 60 by Ande Cook; page 74 by Margeaux Lucas
Interior design by Sandra Harris, Ampersand Design
ISBN: 0-439-48809-5

Table of Contents

~ Introduction ~

Welcome to *The Scholastic Big Book of Holidays Around the Year*! This book was carefully planned and researched to provide you with a wide variety of multicultural and curriculum-based experiences throughout the school year. It contains world religious and cultural holidays, U.S. national holidays, celebrations that salute the contributions of important Americans, plus a variety of educational events to satisfy your classroom needs.

About This Book

★ Sections

This book is divided into three-month seasonal sections: Fall (September–November), Winter (December–February), Spring (March–May), and Summer (June–August). For holidays at a glance, each seasonal section begins with a calendar. If you're looking for a specific holiday but you're unsure of its date, please refer to the index. Reproducible pages corresponding to selected holidays are included at the end of each seasonal section.

★ Holiday Listings

Each holiday heading highlights the name and date of the holiday most widely used in the United States and it territories; names and dates may differ in other countries. The heading also includes the countries and/or religions that celebrate that holiday. Some holidays are celebrated worldwide by people of a certain culture, which are specified (for example, Las Posadas is a Mexican holiday celebrated by Mexicans worldwide as well as in Mexico). Every holiday includes curriculum-based background information, activities, and book links that are adaptable to the age and abilities of your students. For additional holiday-specific resources, see Teacher Resources and Web Links listed throughout the book.

★ Dates of Holidays

The dates of some holidays vary from year to year. For instance, Easter usually falls in April, but sometimes it occurs in March. This is because Easter and many other religious and cultural holidays are based on a lunar calendar that's tied to the appearance of the new moon. Most countries use the solar calendar, called the Gregorian calendar, for daily life and their lunar calendar for dating their religious or historical holidays. Because the moon cycle is shorter than the sun's cycle (by about ten days), the dates on a lunar calendar change from year to year. For the purposes of this book, holidays marked by the lunar calendar are placed in the months in which they most often occur. They also may be cross-referenced in other months.

Many of the major religions have their own lunar calendars; see the explanation of those specific religions on pages 7–10. All lunar calendars except the Islamic calendar adjust periodically to coincide with the solar calendar. (For the history of the solar calendar, see Leap Year Day on page 70.)

You'll also notice that many holidays change dates from year to year. This is because the celebration is scheduled around a special occurrence such as a birthday or anniversary, but the observance is planned for a specific day of the week or month. For instance, Martin Luther King Jr.'s birthday is January 15, but the holiday is scheduled for the second Monday in January.

★ The Holiday Information and Activity Pages

The information and activity ideas for each holiday are organized by the headings listed below.

Information Section

Holiday History: important background on the holiday itself or an aspect of the holiday.

Fast Fact: an interesting piece of trivia for sharing

In Other Words: an explanation or translation of the holiday name or a related term

Traditions Today: how people celebrate the holiday today

America Celebrates: how we celebrate the holiday around the United States

Around the World: how people in other countries celebrate the holiday; special spreads include:

Fall Harvest (November)—includes international party ideas

Holidays of the Christmas Season (December)

Spring Festivals (April)—includes international party ideas

Birthday Rituals (June)

Extending the Information Sections

Excerpt: useful background information straight from the source

Mark Your Calendar: ways to extend the message of the holiday throughout the year

Talk About It: talking points that can be read aloud to students to stimulate discussion

Books and Resources

Book Links: recommended children's books at a variety of levels about the holiday topic

Web Links: great Web sites to use with your lesson

Teacher Resources: useful books and other references on holidays and traditions to aid your instruction

Activities

Most holiday pages offer simple in-class activities that help educate and entertain.

Curriculum Link: a burst naming the curricular focus (social studies, language arts, mathematics, science, art)

Tip: quick help for preparing for the activity and getting it rolling

Bulletin Board Ideas: ways to make an activity come to life on your bulletin board

Reproducible: an introduction to the reproducible page related to the holiday (Reproducibles are located at the end of each seasonal section.)

For Older/Younger Students: ideas for increasing or decreasing the level of difficulty

★ Special Note: Holidays Not Included in This Book

In order to fit the most widely recognized holidays and celebrations with their enriching lessons between the covers of this book, some holidays simply could not be included. If you are looking for more information about a holiday or for a holiday that is not included in this book, please refer to the resources listed below.

Books

Celebrations! Festivals, Carnivals, and Feast Days Around the World
by Barnabas and Anabel Kindersley (DK Publishing, 1997)

Celebrations Around the World: A Multicultural Handbook
by Carole S. Angell (Fulcrum Publishing, 1996)

Chase's Calendar of Events 2002
(McGraw-Hill, 2002)

Ethnic Celebrations Around the World: Festivals, Holidays and Celebrations
by Nancy Everix (Good Apple, 1991)

Hands Around the World: 365 Creative Ways to Build Cultural Awareness and Global Respect
by Susan Milord (Williamson, 1992)

Multicultural Discovery Activities for the Elementary Grades
by Elizabeth Crosby Still (Center for Applied Research in Education, 1995)

What I Believe
by Alan Brown and Andrew Langley (Millbrook Press, 1999)

World Holidays: A Watts Guide for Children
by Heather Moehn (Franklin Watts, 2000)

The World of Festivals
by Philip Steele (Rand McNally, 1997)

Web Sites

Education World: **www.education-world.com**

Holiday Origins: **www.holidayorigins.com**

Scholastic Teacher's Web Site: **www.teacher.scholastic.com**

Yahooligans: **www.yahooligans.com**

★ State Holidays

There's no better way to get to know your state history than by celebrating its holidays. You'll find a handful of state holidays in this book such as Lei Day in Hawaii (page 97), and Utah's Mormon Pioneer Day (page 121). Unfortunately, there isn't enough room for the thorough coverage they deserve. If you'd like to find out more about your state's holidays or start your own state holiday curriculum, consult the InfoPlease Web site at **www.infoplease.com** and search under state holidays.

Holidays and Multicultural Appreciation

Your students may come from many different backgrounds, and they may practice different religions. This book provides you and your class with information and resources for learning about many holidays observed by the major religions. The inclusion of religious holidays, of course, serves an educational rather than a religious purpose. The activities paired with these holidays focus on cultural aspects of the holiday, so that students may better appreciate and respect diverse religious traditions. Tailor your teaching about these holidays in a way that you feel is appropriate for the age and backgrounds of your students.

Some religious groups, such as Jehovah's Witnesses, do not recognize any celebration days —religious and national holidays, birthdays, and so on. Students who practice as Jehovah's Witnesses will abstain from all holiday activities. You might want to speak with these students and their families about exposure to holiday celebrations (including birthday parties). With a little creative planning, you can find a balance between their religious needs and the social and academic experiences of the rest of your students. Consider, for example, setting up an enjoyable activity for these students, such as reading aloud to younger students in another class during Halloween festivities and creating a corner for crafts or educational games during other celebrations in the classroom.

For more information, see "Religious Holiday Activity Guidelines" in the teachers' section of the Anti-Defamation League's Web site at **www.adl.org**.

★ Religions and Their Holidays

Some of the holidays in this book are associated with one or more religions. Background on the major world religions appears below. For more information on these or other religions that could not be included, consult the sources listed at the end of the section.

Judaism

The Jewish faith began more than 4,000 years ago in the Middle East at a time when people worshiped many different gods. A man named Abraham believed in one god. God called Abraham and Abraham's descendents his Chosen People and led them into Canaan.

Types: Orthodox, Conservative, Reform

Students' observances: Some Jewish boys may wear yarmulkes (YAH-muh-kahz) on their heads to show respect for God. Students who keep kosher follow dietary restrictions, including not eating pork or shellfish, and not eating meat and dairy products from the same dish or during the same meal.

Religious education: Many Jewish children go to Hebrew school classes at their temples, starting in early elementary grades. At the age of twelve (girls) and thirteen (boys), some participate in a bat mitzvah (girls) or bar mitzvah (boys) ceremony that welcomes them into the adult community.

Main holidays: Rosh Hashanah in September/October (page 18), Yom Kippur in September/October (page 18), Hanukkah in December (page 46), and Passover in March/April (page 84).

Calendar: Jewish holidays are scheduled according to a special lunar calendar invented more than 2,300 years ago. Year 1, the date of creation, corresponds with 3761 B.C. in the Gregorian calendar, so the year A.D. 2000 is year 5761 in the Jewish calendar. The twelve months alternate between twenty-nine and thirty days in length. To adjust the calendar, a thirteenth month is

added seven times within a cycle of nineteen years. The Jewish calendar starts at Rosh Hashanah, the Jewish New Year, which falls in September or October. The months of the calendar are Tishri, Heshvan, Kislev, Tebet, Shebat, Adar, Nisan, Iyar, Sivan, Tammuz, Ab, Elul.

Christianity

Christians follow the teachings of Jesus Christ, a Jew who was born about 2,000 years ago in what is now Israel. Christians believe that Jesus is the son of God who came to Earth to show God's love. They believe that God comes to people in three ways called the trinity: the Father, the Son (Jesus), and the Holy Spirit.

Types: There are many Christian groups, including Roman Catholic, Protestant (Presbyterian, Methodist), Orthodox Christian, Unitarian, and various sects (Mormon, Jehovah's Witness).

Students' observances: There are few dietary restrictions in the Christian faith. During Lent, Catholics are asked to give up something meaningful to them, such as candy or sweets. Also many Catholic families choose not to eat meat on Fridays. Jehovah's Witnesses do not celebrate any holidays, including birthdays.

Religious education: Many Christian students attend weekly Sunday school to learn about their faith. Catholic students attend catechism classes to prepare for their first Holy Communion at around the age of seven. In this church ceremony, children first take the bread and wine that symbolize the body and blood of Christ.

Main holidays: Advent and Christmas in December (pages 49–50); the forty days of Lent in February/March/April (pages 69–70); Holy Week and Easter in March/April (pages 85–86). People around the world celebrate certain saints' days, including All Souls' Day and All Saints' Day in November (page 28), Day of Our Lady of Guadalupe in December (page 48), and St. Patrick's Day in March (page 83).

Calendar: The forty days of Lent ending with Easter Sunday are the only Christian holidays scheduled on the lunar cycle. As established by the Council of Nicaea in the year A.D. 325, Easter Sunday can occur between March 22 and April 25; it is celebrated on the first Sunday after the full moon that occurs on or after the vernal equinox on March 21. After that date is established, count forty days (or seven Wednesdays and excluding Sundays) back to Ash Wednesday, which is the beginning of Lent.

Islam

Muslims, the followers of Islam, believe in one god called Allah. Muslims believe that Allah sent prophets to teach his laws. The Qur'an (Koran) is the Arabic holy book containing the words of Allah revealed to the prophet Muhammad.

Types: The majority of Muslims are Sunnis; smaller groups are Shi'as and Sufis. The Nation of Islam is an African-American Muslim group first organized in the 1930s.

Students' observances: Most Muslims in America wear western clothes. The Qur'an simply states that Muslims dress modestly. Pork and alcohol are forbidden in Islam. During the entire month of Ramadan, Muslims fast from sunrise to sunset.

Religious education: Some Muslim students take evening lessons at their local mosque to learn the Qur'an.

Main holidays: Ramadan and Eid-al-Fitr (page 34); others include Eid-al-Adha ("feast of sacrifice") and Maulid al Nabi (Muhammad's birthday).

Calendar: The Islamic (or Hijri) calendar began on July 16, 622 (A.D., Gregorian calendar), when the prophet Muhammad went into exile in Medina. It is solely a lunar calendar based on the phases of the moon, with no adjustments made to the solar calendar. Because of this, the calendar moves back ten or eleven days each year. That's why Muslim holidays can fall in any season of the year. The Islamic calendar months are Muharram, Safar, Rabi' al-awwal, Rabi' al-thani, Jumada al-awwal, Jumada al-thani, Rajab, Shaban, Ramadan, Shawwal, Dhu al-Qi'dah, Dh al-Hijja.

Hinduism

Hinduism includes many ancient beliefs and customs. The religion has no bible, but it has many books of stories, hymns, and prayers. Hindus believe in many gods who walk the earth as people and animals; they are all different forms of one supreme god. Hindus believe in reincarnation after death (that they will be born again).

Students' observances: Most Hindus are vegetarian.

Main holidays: Diwali in October/November (page 21), Holi in late February/March (page 97), and Krishna Janmastami in August/September (page 121).

Calendar: The Hindu calendar, or the Indian National Calendar, is based on a lunar and solar calendar. It has twelve months of thirty days, or 360 days. To adjust, a leap month is added every five years. The months, all starting with the emergence of the full moon, have two parts: Krsna, when the moon is getting smaller (waning), and Suklan, when the moon is getting fuller (waxing). The Hindu calendar starts in March or April. The months are Chaitra, Vaisakha, Jyaistha, Asadha, Sravana, Bhadrapada, Asvina, Kartika, Margasirsa, Pausa, Magha, Phalguna.

Sikhism

Sikhism is a religion founded in north India. Sikhs believe in one god as taught by Guru Nanak and other gurus (teachers) according to the holy book Guru Granth Sahib. They also believe in reincarnation, or rebirth.

Religious education: When Sikh children are fifteen years old, they can join the khalsa, the Sikh community. Amrit is the ceremony in which they promise to follow Sikh teachings. After this, men leave their hair and beard long and follow other dress codes to show their faith.

Main holidays: Guru Nanak's Birthday in October/November (page 33); Sikhs also observe their own versions of the Hindu holidays Diwali in October (page 21) and Holi in February/March (page 97).

Calendar: The Nanakshahi calendar is based on the length of the tropical solar year instead of the lunar cycle so the dates do not fluctuate. The Sikh new year begins on March 14. The months are Chet (March 14), Vaisakh (April 14), Jeth (May 15), Harh (June 15), Sawan (July 16), Bhadon (August 16), Asu (September 15), Katik (October 15), Maghar (November 14), Poh (December 14), Magh (January 13), Phagan (February 12).

Buddhism

Buddhists follow the teachings of Siddhartha Gautama, known as the Buddha. They do not believe in gods but seek enlightenment or nirvana. Buddhists believe that everyone has many lives and many deaths. One of Buddhism's great teachers today is the Dalai Lama.

Types: Buddhists live around the world, but most are in Asian countries such as Nepal, Tibet, China, Japan, Thailand, India, and Sri Lanka. Each country observes unique festivals.

Religious education: To help reach enlightenment, in some countries boys and girls go away for a short time to become monks and nuns, respectively. A boy's head is shaved, and he wears an orange or red robe.

Students' observances: The youngest Buddhists are urged to learn to meditate.

Main holidays: Buddha's Birthday in April (page 89) and Buddhist New Year in April (Songkran in Thailand, page 97).

Calendar: The Buddhist calendar is different in various parts of the world. The most common one is a lunar calendar that begins roughly in December or January. Each month is twenty-nine or thirty days in length. Every few years, an extra leap day is added to the end of the seventh month. Every nineteen years, an extra month is added to the seventh month as well. In most countries, months are known only as numbers (first month or moon).

Resources

The Everything World's Religions Book: Discover the Beliefs, Traditions, and Cultures of Ancient and Modern Religions
by Robert Pollack (Adams Media, 2002)

What I Believe: A Young Person's Guide to the Religions of the World
by Alan Brown and Andrew Langley (Millbrook Press, 1999)

World Holidays: A Watts Guide for Children
by Heather Moehn (Franklin Watts, 2000)

Fall Calendar

September

First Monday in September	LABOR DAY	United States, Canada	12
September 9	KITE FESTIVAL	China	13
September 11	SEPTEMBER 11	United States, worldwide	14
September 15–October 15	HISPANIC HERITAGE MONTH	United States	15
September 17	CITIZENSHIP DAY	United States	17
September or October	THE HIGH HOLY DAYS: ROSH HASHANAH & YOM KIPPUR	Jewish	18
September 19	FEAST OF SAN GENNARO	Italian/Christian	19
September 28	CONFUCIUS'S BIRTHDAY	Asia	19

October

First Monday in October	CHILD HEALTH DAY	United States	20
Date varies (sometimes in September)	OKTOBERFEST	German	21
Date varies (sometimes in November)	DIWALI	Hindu	21
Second Monday in October	COLUMBUS DAY	United States and other countries in the Americas	22
Week of October 9	FIRE PREVENTION WEEK	United States	23
October 31	HALLOWEEN	United States, United Kingdom, Canada, other countries	24
Harvest Season	FALL HARVESTS AROUND THE WORLD	Barbados, Hong Kong, Vietnam, Thailand, Native American, Zambia, India, Ghana	26

November

October 31–November 2	THE DAY OF THE DEAD (EL DIA DE LOS MUERTOS)	Mexico, Latin America, Spain (Christian)	28
November 1–30	NATIONAL AMERICAN INDIAN HERITAGE MONTH	United States	29
Tuesday after first Monday in November	ELECTION DAY	United States	31
November 11	VETERANS DAY	United States, Canada, Australia	32
November 18	GURU NANAK'S BIRTHDAY	Sikh	33
November 21	WORLD HELLO DAY	Worldwide	33
November/date varies	RAMADAN	Muslim	34
Third week in November	NATIONAL CHILDREN'S BOOK WEEK	United States	35
Last Thursday in November	THANKSGIVING	United States	36

Fall Reproducibles

For great ideas for celebrating students' birthdays, see Birthday Celebrations Around the World in June on page 117.

Labor Day

First Monday of September • United States and Canada

Labor Day pays tribute to American workers. Take this opportunity to teach students about the history of labor and about jobs today.

★ Book Link

Jobs People Do by Christopher Maynard (DK Publishing, 1997). Picture book, all ages. Children demonstrate all kinds of work and responsibilities.

★ Web Link

Visit the Department of Labor's Web site to find the Fair Labor Standards Act at **www.dol.gov/esa/whd/**.

~ EXCERPT ~

To help students understand the concept of unions, ask: "What's your job?" (Typical answers include "to go to school" and "to do what my teacher tells me to do.") "If you do good work, you're supposed to get good grades. But if you did 'A' work and got all 'F's, would that be fair? What could you do about it?" Make the point that working adults form unions because unions work to make sure their members, and all workers, are treated fairly.

—from AFL-CIO's "Talking Union to Your Kids" at **www.aflcio.org** (2000)

Holiday History *Read Aloud*

When the Central Labor Union of New York City was formed in 1882, the workers and their families were very excited. They held a big festival on September 5. The workers marched in a parade. Carpenters, bricklayers, and other tradespeople carried their tools and banners for their unions. Thousands of people stood at the curbs to watch. The celebration continued with a huge picnic and fireworks.

In Other Words *Read Aloud*

A union is a gathering of people. A labor union is a gathering of workers. Why do workers need to gather together, or unionize? When workers unionize, they have one strong voice. They can ask for things they need, and their bosses will listen. The first labor unions in America fought hard and won important rights for workers, such as safer working conditions and fair pay.

Fast Fact *Read Aloud*

Did you ever wonder why your parents work, but you don't? About a hundred years ago, children in the United States did work. They picked cotton, canned fish, and made clothes in factories. Breaker boys were young children at mines who pulled rocks and slate from passing coal cars. The hours were long, pay was low, and the work was dangerous. In 1938, the Fair Labor Standards Act was created to protect children from dangerous work. Now, a person younger than sixteen years old can't have a job in the United States.

Talk About It In some countries, there are still no laws protecting child workers. How would you feel if you had to work all day long?

Traditions Today

Labor Day has become the symbolic end of summer. For many Americans, it's a time to go on vacation or simply relax at home. Then it's time to return to work and school and await the beginning of fall.

Kite Festival

Ninth day of ninth month of the Chinese calendar (sometimes September 9) • China

Enjoy the spectacle of kite flying while sharing an Asian tradition.

In Other Words

The Kite Festival is also called the Double Nine Festival because it falls on the ninth day of the ninth month.

Make the Dates `Math`

Quiz students on the months of the year and their corresponding numbers. Show that dates can be written in several different ways. For instance, September 8, 2000, is also 9/8/00. In Europe, the same date would be written as 08.09.00. Have students write their birth dates in different ways.

★ **Book Link**

Easy-to-Make Decorative Kites by Alan Bridgewater (Dover, 1988). Picture book, all ages. Directions for creating kites from around the world.

Fast Fact

The Chinese holiday calendar is based on the cycles of the moon. Each year of this traditional lunar calendar has about twelve months. Each month begins at a new moon, so it is twenty-nine or thirty days long. To stay adjusted to our solar calendar, the Chinese calendar adds a month after the seventh month every nineteen years. For more information about the lunar calendar, see page 4.

Holiday History *Read Aloud*

During the Kite Festival, kites of all shapes, sizes, and colors fill the sky from morning to night. When did the first kite fly in China? According to legend, around 200 B.C. Han Shin made the first kites and used them in battle. He put whistles on giant kites and flew them over his enemy's camp. The strange sight and noises scared the enemy forces. (See Asian-Pacific American Heritage Month, pages 94–95, for more about Asian kite-flying games.)

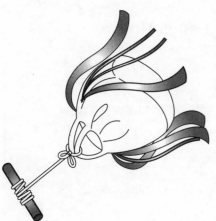

Fly a Kite! `Art`

Students can create a simple kite out of a grocery bag, string, and common craft materials.

★ Staple decorative streamers and ribbons to the outside of a plastic grocery bag without stapling it closed.
★ Tie the handles together with one end of a 10-foot length of string.
★ Tie the other end of the string to a short dowel (about 6 inches long). Wind the string around the dowel to create a spool to hold.
★ Run! The wind will fill the bag with air and make it soar.

September 11

September 11 • Worldwide

On this tragic anniversary, discuss the concepts of hate and fear, hope and peace—and emphasize the importance of building community.

★ Book Links

Children's Prayers for America edited by Karlynn Keys Lee (Northland Publishing, 2001). Picture book, all ages. Contains children's artwork and messages of peace in the aftermath of September 11.

Messages to Ground Zero: Children Respond to September 11, 2001 by Shelley Harwayne/ New York City Board of Education (Heinemann, 2002). Picture book, all ages. Letters, poems, and artwork by children in New York City and across the country in response to the September 11 tragedy.

A Nation Challenged by the staff of *The New York Times* (Scholastic, 2002). Reference book, intermediate. Account of the events of September 11, the war in Afghanistan, and security measures at home and abroad with Pulitzer Prize-winning photography.

★ Web Link

The Anti-Defamation League Web site at **www.adl.org** has a wide range of articles to help you broach topics such as hatred and prejudice.

Holiday History

On September 11, 2001, terrorists hijacked planes and struck the World Trade Center in New York City and the Pentagon in Washington, D.C. Another plane crashed in Pennsylvania. Thousands of civilians, firefighters, and police officers were killed during the tragedy and the rescue.

Unity Quilt `Social Studies`   `Math`

Promote tolerance and unity in your classroom by creating a classroom unity quilt. Distribute squares of construction paper and have students write and illustrate a short poem or statement about their feelings, fears, and hopes for the world. Some starters might include "I imagine a world…," "I used to… but now I…," "I wish…," "If only…." Integrate math concepts by alternating colored squares in patterns of 2, 3, or 4 and by having students manipulate the square units to create rectangular quilts of different dimensions. They can determine perimeter and area as well.

~ EXCERPT ~

In discussing the events of September 11 with students,

★ Review what actually happened (the general facts).

★ Share your perceptions of the situation and your feelings about it. It is important to keep perspective here so students are not overwhelmed.

★ Let students know that many people share their concern and that people may show that concern in a variety of ways, with different feelings and reactions.

★ Emphasize that there are organizations that are helping people who were hurt or lost loved ones, jobs, and homes and are keeping us safe: the president and Congress, the police, the Red Cross, and other government and civic groups.

★ Let them know that while there are people who do things that are hard to understand, we live in a wonderful country and, for the most part, we are all safe.

★ Now listen to students: What questions do they have for you? How are they feeling? For younger students, do not give more specific detail than necessary. See what, if any, questions they have so you can judge what they need from you. Give them reassurance.

—adapted from "Discussing Hate and Violence with Your Children" by Dr. Donald J. Cohen, director of Yale Child Study Center and professor of child psychiatry, pediatrics and psychology at Yale University, at **www.adl.org**

Hispanic Heritage Month

September 15–October 15 • United States

Celebrate the Latino heritage of your students and our country. The festivities begin in the middle of September when independence days in Mexico and Central America are observed.

Around The World

On a world map, identify Mexico, Puerto Rico, Cuba, Spain, Portugal, the nations in Central America and South America, and some islands in the Caribbean. Explain that many people living in the United States came here from these countries.

★Talk About ★It Have you ever visited a Spanish-speaking country? If so, what was the purpose of your visit—to see relatives, to take a vacation? How is the place you visited different from your hometown? How is it the same?

Fast Fact

Spanish is spoken by 332 million people around the world! Celebrate Hispanic Heritage Month by teaching some basic Spanish to students or inviting Spanish-speaking students to introduce some of their favorite words or idiomatic expressions to the class. Use a beginner's Spanish dictionary as a resource.

Holiday History ★Read Aloud★

Many delicious foods we eat come from Hispanic countries. One example is chocolate, made from cocoa beans, which the Incas, Mayas, and Aztecs in Central and South America grew. These flavorful beans chiefly grow in Ecuador, Brazil, and other Central and South American countries.

★Talk About ★It What are some other favorite foods you might find in Hispanic restaurants?

In Other Words

The first chocolate wasn't sweet at all! The Mayas and Aztecs roasted cocoa beans from the cacao tree for a drink called *xocoatl*—pronounced "SHOH-koh-tel"—which means "bitter water."

¡Chocolate!, page 39 `Social Studies`

Enjoy this recipe for chocolate caliente while teaching students a traditional Spanish chant. FOR OLDER STUDENTS: Let students choose a country to learn about by filling in their names on a reproducible map of Mexico and Central and South America. Have them write a short report on that country's culture and food. Hold a Latin American Feast Day and encourage students to bring in a dish or pass out a recipe card for a dish that is native to the country they chose.

★ **Book Links**

Author/illustrator **Lulu Delacre** specializes in making Hispanic folktales come to life.

Arroz con Leche: Popular Songs and Rhymes from Latin America (Scholastic, 1992). Picture book, easy. Children learn simple verses in English and Spanish from many countries.

The Bossy Gallito retold by Lucia M. Gonzales (Scholastic, 1999). Picture book, easy. This traditional Cuban tale includes a Spanish translation.

Golden Tales: Myths, Legends and Folktales From Latin America (Scholastic, 2001). Picture book, intermediate. This collection is great for older students.

★ **Teacher Resource**

The Teachers Resource Center on the Scholastic Web site features biographies and book links for Delacre and many other writers and illustrators. Check it out at **www.teacher.scholastic.com**.

Reproducible

Chocolate Caliente *(Hot Chocolate)*

★ 8 squares (8 ounces) sweetened chocolate
★ 4 cups skim milk
★ 4 drops vanilla extract
★ cinnamon

Break chocolate into small pieces. Combine chocolate, milk, and vanilla in a saucepan, constantly stirring. Bring to a boil. Use a whisk to mix it. Pour into cups. Sprinkle cinnamon on top. Serves 4–6 people.

Hispanic Heritage Month

★ Book Links

Say Hola to Spanish by Susan Middleton Elya (Scholastic, 1998). Picture book, easiest. This rhyming picture book makes basic Spanish easy.

Abuela by Arthur Dorros (Dutton, 1997). Picture book, all ages. As Rosalba imagines flying over Manhattan with her grandmother, students learn simple Spanish words and phrases.

★ Teacher Resource

Celebrations Around the World: A Multicultural Handbook by Carole S. Angell (Fulcrum, 1996). All grades. Compendium of holidays with related games and activities.

Spanish Surprise Language Arts

★ Post a Spanish word of the day on the board or chart paper. Review its spelling and pronunciation.

★ Whenever anyone says the English word, students raise their hands and call out "Sorpresa!" (Surprise!). The first student to raise his or her hand can say the Spanish word.

★ At the end of the day, have students add the word to their list of "Spanish Words We Know." FOR YOUNGER STUDENTS: Students can write each word in both languages and draw a picture of it. FOR OLDER STUDENTS: Students can define the word and include its pronunciation. They will be surprised at how many words they remember at the end of the month!

Here are 14 words you might use for this activity:

hola	(OH-lah)	hello
el Español	(ES-pah-NYOHL)	Spanish
la escuela	(ess-KWAY-lah)	school
el maestro	(mah-ESS-stroh)	teacher (male)
la maestra	(mah-ESS-strah)	teacher (female)
el alumno	(ah-LOOM-noh)	student (male)
la alumna	(ah-LOOM-nah)	student (female)
los Estados Unidos	(ess-TAH-dohs oo-NEE-dohs)	the United States
el lápiz	(LAH-pees)	pencil, crayon
la pluma	(PLOO-mah)	pen
rojo	(ROH-hoh)	red
adios	(ah-DYOS)	good-bye

 America Celebrates

Many cities have Spanish names: Los Angeles and San Antonio to name just a few! What cities in your state have Spanish names? Do any streets in your town have Spanish names? Find out if the name has a special meaning.

La Thunka Social Studies   Language Arts

La Thunka is a hopscotch-type game from Bolivia.

★ Draw a hopscotch board. Write the Spanish names of the days of the week in the spaces—Lunes, Martes, Miércoles, Jueves, Viernes, Sábado, and Domingo (Monday through Sunday).

★ Each player tosses a flat stone onto each day in turn, hops to that square on one foot, and (with the other foot) kicks the stone over the starting line.

★ Players continue until they make a mistake, such as missing the appropriate square, putting the other foot down, or failing to kick the stone over the starting line.

★ The first player to reach Domingo (Sunday) is the winner.

—adapted from *Celebrations Around the World: A Multicultural Handbook*

Citizenship Day

September 17 • United States

On September 17, 1787, our forefathers signed the Constitution after the defeat of the British in the American Revolution. This important document made us a free country and gave us many rights as citizens. Choose this day to celebrate U.S. citizenship and discuss the privileges of citizens.

Fast Fact *Read Aloud*

We have special rights as U.S. citizens. For example, we can practice any religion—that's why Americans may be Christian, Jewish, Muslim, Buddhist, or any other religion they choose. By voting, we also have the right to decide who will lead our government. You can vote when you reach the age of 18.

Talk About It How would life be different in the United States if we didn't have these rights?

Mark Your Calendar

Teach students about voting and the election process. For more information, see Election Day in November on page 31.

Traditions Today *Read Aloud*

On Citizenship Day, immigrants, or people who were born in another country, can become U.S. citizens. They must be at least eighteen years old and have lived in the United States for five years. After passing a special test about our government and history, they become citizens in a special ceremony. They take an oath of allegiance—a promise to be good and dedicated citizens of our country.

Citizenship Test, page 40   Social Studies

What does it mean to be a citizen of a country? Why might you need to take a test? Challenge students to answer questions from the Citizenship Test. (Answers appear on page 126.) FOR YOUNGER STUDENTS: Although this is a tough test for young students, the answers are still important; try taking the test together. Multiple-choice answers provide discussion points. A good way to help young students understand some of these concepts is to relate questions to your classroom—for instance, talk about how democracy works in your classroom, make a class flag, and so on.

Reproducible

★ Book Links

We the Kids illustrated by David Catrow (Penguin Putnam, 2002). Picture book, all ages. Explains how the preamble to the Constitution applies to a child's world.

Shh! We're Writing the Constitution by Jean Fritz (Putnam, 1998). Chapter book with pictures, intermediate. The details in this book are just right for older students, and Tomie DePaola's drawings keep it entertaining.

I Was Dreaming to Come to America: Memories from the Ellis Island Oral History Project selected and illustrated by Veronica Lawlor (Penguin, 1997). Picture book, all ages. Contains short but poignant quotes from immigrants.

The Pledge of Allegiance (Cartwheel, 2001). Picture book, all ages. Commemorative edition featuring photos of children and places around our country.

★ Teacher Resource

Immigration Then and Now: Background Information, Audiotape, Literature Links, Poster, Activities by Karen Baicker (Scholastic, 1997). For grades 4–8.

High Holy Days
Rosh Hashanah and Yom Kippur

September or October (the first ten days of Tishri on the Jewish calendar) • Jews worldwide

Share the rich traditions and the message of the first ten days of the Jewish New Year.

For more about Judaism and the Jewish calendar, see page 7.

★ Book Links

Gershon's Monster: The Story of the Jewish New Year retold by Eric A. Kimmel (Scholastic, 2000). Picture book, all ages. A traditional story about starting anew, with beautiful illustrations by Jon J. Muth.

Sound the Shofar by Leslie Kimmelman (HarperCollins, 1998). Picture book, all ages. Take a walk through the rituals of the High Holy Days with a contemporary family.

Holiday History ✳Read Aloud✳

The High Holy Days are the first ten days of the Jewish New Year. The first day is Rosh Hashanah, "the head of the year." During Rosh Hashanah and over the next ten days, Jewish people apologize for their mistakes and ask for forgiveness. The tenth day, Yom Kippur, is the day for cleansing—for getting rid of sins for the year. Jewish people cleanse themselves spiritually by fasting, or not eating, for one day. People who are thirteen years and older must fast; younger children do their part by skipping breakfast.

In Other Words

Le Shanah tovah! (leh SHAH-nah TOE-vah!) is the Hebrew greeting used to celebrate Rosh Hashanah. It means, "May it be a good and sweet year."

Fast Fact ✳Read Aloud✳

We blow noisemakers to bring in the New Year. On Rosh Hashanah, it's traditional to blow a shofar, a ram's horn. This 3,000-year-old musical instrument has a loud and startling sound. Long ago, it was used to call people together in times of trouble. Now the shofar is used to say, "Wake up!" to remind people to do better.

Traditions Today

The Rosh Hashanah meal traditionally includes challah, a sweet bread, and pieces of apple for dipping into honey. Families wish for a "sweet" year to come.

HONEY

America Celebrates ✳Read Aloud✳

At sundown on Yom Kippur, some Jewish families will hold a "break fast" gathering—a time for friends and family to come to their home to break the fast together. The family will serve light foods that are easy to digest such as bagels and cream cheese, whitefish salad, and deli meats on rye bread.

Feast of San Gennaro

September 19 • Italians worldwide/Christian

Ciao! Explore some Italian history and traditions as you celebrate this popular holiday.

Holiday History

San Gennaro, also known as St. Januarius, was an Italian bishop who lived nearly 2,000 years ago. Called "the protector of Naples," San Gennaro was killed because he was outspoken about his religious beliefs. A vial of his blood remains in the Italian city of Naples. It is believed to miraculously become liquid on the anniversary of San Gennaro's death. People believe that if the blood doesn't liquefy, Naples will have bad luck.

America Celebrates

The San Gennaro Festival is a happy event for Italian Americans. The biggest festival is an eleven-day event held in Little Italy in New York City. It begins with a parade led by a statue of Saint Gennaro. A big street fair follows with games, rides, and food—sausage sandwiches with sliced onions and green peppers are a special favorite. Buon appetito!

In Other Words

Buon appetito (BWON ah-peh-TEE-toh) means "enjoy your meal" in Italian. Here's how to pronounce the Italian words for some common foods.

il pane	(PAH-nay)	bread
il latte	(LAH-tay)	milk
il formaggio	(for-MAHD-joh)	cheese
le frutta	(FROO-tah)	fruit
il gelato	(jeh-LAH-toh)	ice cream

Confucius's Birthday

September 28 • Asians worldwide

Asian philosopher Confucius was born around 551 B.C. His timeless teachings provide a basis for age-appropriate discussions about respect, duty, and self-discipline.

Holiday History *Read Aloud*

Confucius never wrote down his teachings, but his followers did. After Confucius's death, they collected his philosophies in a book called the *Analects*. Here are a few of his sayings:

★ Do not impose on others what you do not wish for yourself.

★ Do not worry when people fail to recognize your merits. Worry when you fail to recognize theirs.

★ An exemplary person helps bring out what is beautiful in other people and discourages what is ugly in them. A petty person does just the opposite.

Talk About It Confucius's thoughts on respect for others are the basis of the Golden Rule: "Do unto others, as you would have them do unto you." What does the Golden Rule mean? What are the "Golden Rules" in your classroom?

★ Book Link

Confucius: The Golden Rule by Russell Freedman (Scholastic, 2002). Chapter book, intermediate. This biography of Confucius features breathtaking paintings by Frédéric Clément that depict various passages from the *Analects*.

Traditions Today

In Asia, Confucius's birthday is Teachers' Day, a day to celebrate all teachers and their contributions to society. Some communities hold festivals with traditions that are more than 2,000 years old.

Child Health Day

First Monday in October • United States

Devote this day to reviewing healthy habits and learning about how the body works.

Good Health Talks   `Science`

Invite special guests to your class to discuss health issues and give tips.

School Nurse
- cleanliness (wash hands after eating, care for cuts)
- good hygiene (bathing, toilet behavior, blowing nose)
- importance of drinking water, especially on hot days

Gym Teacher or Fitness Instructor
- exercise, including warm up and cool down
- taking good care of lungs and muscles

Pediatrician
- common communicable diseases (colds, flu) and their causes
- importance of staying home when you're sick

Dentist
- brushing and flossing teeth
- eating proper foods

Eye Doctor
- why you need glasses
- types of eye diseases

Nutritionist
- the food groups
- proper diet and vitamins

Food Pyramid on a Plate   `Science`

Put the message of eating healthy on a plate! On the board or chart paper, draw a simple food pyramid like the one shown, or download it from the USDA Web site at **www.usda.gov**. Have students use colored markers to copy the food pyramid on a white or light-colored paper plate, and write and draw examples of foods they eat from each group in the appropriate sections. Cover the finished plate with a clear, reusable plastic plate of the same size to preserve the picture. Use clear tape to hold the plates together. FOR YOUNGER STUDENTS: Create a triangle template with four lines dividing it into sections as shown. Label the sections by food group. Reproduce the template, distribute copies, and have students draw one example from each food group in the appropriate section. Have them cut out their food pyramid and glue it to the paper plate.

Food pyramid:
- fats, oils, sweets • use sparingly •
- milk, yogurt, cheese • 2–3 Servings •
- meat, poultry, fish, beans, eggs, nuts • 2–3 Servings •
- vegetables • 3–5 Servings •
- fruit • 2–4 Servings •
- bread, rice, cereal, pasta • 6–11 Servings •

★ Book Links

Body Battles by Rita Golden Gelman (Scholastic, 1992). Chapter book with illustrations, all ages. The body fights off harmful disease thanks to mucus, cilia, earwax, stomach acid, and more. This book includes a very strong (but kid-friendly) message about avoiding drugs.

Healthy Me: Fun Ways to Develop Good Health and Safety Habits by Michelle O'Brien-Palmer (Chicago Review Press, 1999). Chapter book with illustrations, all ages. Health and safety lessons are presented through fun projects, games, and experiments.

Eat Healthy, Feel Great by William Sears. M.D., Martha Sears, R.N., and Christie Watts Kelly (Little, Brown, 2002). Picture book, all ages. Readers learn why they are what they eat.

★ Web Link

It's never too early to talk about the dangers of cigarettes, drugs, alcohol, and harmful chemicals. Check out "Talking With Kids About Alcohol and Drugs" at **www.talkingwithkids.org**. The content is geared toward parents, but it's useful for teachers as well.

Oktoberfest

Date varies in October (sometimes in September) • Germans worldwide

Enjoy German traditions while celebrating this fun and festive holiday.

Holiday History *Read Aloud*

The first Oktoberfest was held in 1810 to celebrate the marriage of King Ludwig I of Bavaria to Princess Therese von Sachsen Hillburghausen. Germany's most famous festival, Oktoberfest features fairs and parades, dancers and singers, food and drink. The festival at the Theresa Meadows fairgrounds in Munich, Germany's capital, attracts huge crowds.

America Celebrates

Many U.S. cities with large German-American populations—such as Tulsa, Oklahoma, and Carson City, Nevada—celebrate Oktoberfest. People dance the polka to German oompah bands.

Story and a Snack `Language Arts`

Read aloud tales by the Brothers Grimm, the most famous of Germany's storytellers. Snack on traditional treats such as pretzels and gingerbread cookies.

★ Book Link

Hansel and Gretel, *Rumpelstilskin*, and *Rapunzel* retold by Rika Lesser (Penguin Putnam, 1984). Picture books, all ages. The traditional Brothers Grimm stories with award-winning illustrations by Paul O. Zelinsky.

Diwali

Date varies in October or November (last two days of Asvina and first two of Kartika on the Hindu calendar) • Hindus worldwide

Explore the wonders of light in the Hindu tradition.

Holiday History *Read Aloud*

Diwali, the Hindu New Year, is known as the Festival of Lights. The light celebrates the triumph of good over evil. It is said that on this day Rama, the hero of an Indian tale, returned to his people after winning a fight against the demon king Ravana. In India and other countries, people who practice Hinduism place candles or hang small clay lanterns called diyas inside and outside their homes. The holiday occurs in the fall on the new moon, when the sky is darkest, so the illuminated homes brighten the night.

For more about Hinduism and the Hindu calendar, see page 9.

In Other Words

Diwali is known as the Festival of Lights. Sometimes called Deepaawali or Deepavali, it literally means array (vali) of lamps (deep).

Diwali Night in a Box `Science`

What does a night scene look like in India during Diwali? To simulate the effects of dots of light in the darkness, try this simple demonstration. Paint the inside of a shoebox black (or line it with black construction paper). Poke a few tiny holes in the top and sides with a pin. Cut a half-inch round hole in the side of the box with scissors and insert a drinking straw. Attach the top to the shoebox with masking tape. Have students look through the straw—they should see dots of lights in the darkness. Poke more holes or enlarge the holes with a pencil tip to add more light.

Columbus Day

Second Monday in October • United States and the Americas

Although controversy exists about the importance and integrity of Columbus's voyage, this holiday is useful in introducing the topics of exploration and discovery.

★ Book Links

Christopher Columbus by Stephen Krensky (Random House, 1991). Picture book, easy. The story of Columbus's voyage presented in an early-reading format.

In Their Own Words: Christopher Columbus by Peter and Connie Roop (Scholastic, 2000). Chapter book, intermediate. Columbus's personal journal reveals the details of his exploration.

Encounter by Jane Yolen (Harcourt, 1996). Picture book, all ages. A thought-provoking account of Columbus's discovery told from the perspective of a Taino boy.

★ Web Link

Learn more about longitude and explorations on the Study Works! Web site at **www.studyworksonline.com**. Try Anchors Aweigh, a longitude mapping game.

★ Teacher Resource

50 Thematic Songs Sung to Your Favorite Tunes by Meish Goldish (Scholastic, 1999). For grades K–2.

★Reproducible★

Holiday History

In 1492, the Italian explorer Christopher Columbus was sent by the king and queen of Spain to find a western passage to Japan and the East Indies. He set sail with three ships—the *Niña*, the *Pinta*, and the *Santa María*. On October 12, Columbus landed on Watling Island in San Salvador and claimed the territory for Spain. He made three more voyages that toured many islands off the coast of North America. Ironically, Columbus never knew of the importance of his voyage to European exploration; until his death, he believed he had reached the East Indies.

In Other Words

The misnomer "Indians" came from Christopher Columbus. Since he believed he was in the Indies, he called the native people Indians.

Fast Fact

A simple miscalculation in longitude brought Columbus to America's shores. Longitude lines run north–south on our maps of Earth, and are farthest apart at the equator. In Columbus's day, not much was known about longitude. He thought it was 2,278 miles west from Spain to Asia; in fact, it's about 9,000 miles.

Go Global With Time Zones   `Science`   `Math`

Use longitude to teach about time zones. On a world map, point out the Prime Meridian at Greenwich, England, and the 23 other longitude lines around the world. Explain that each line represents an hour since it takes Earth 24 hours to rotate on its axis. Show the longitude lines that divide the United States into the eastern, central, mountain, and pacific time zones. What time is it in Los Angeles when it's noon in New York? Test with different cities in the United States and around the world.

Columbus Sing-Along, page 41   `Social Studies`

Teach students about Christopher Columbus's journey through song. Add hand and body movements for the chorus lines. For instance, move arms like waves with "sail on, sail on." FOR OLDER STUDENTS: Make up new verses!

Traditions Today

The celebration of Columbus's voyage and his "discovery" have been called into question by the argument that Native Americans inhabited America long before he arrived. Encourage students to discuss this issue and explore the heritage of Native Americans. For activities, see National American Indian Heritage Month in November on pages 29–30.

Fire Prevention Week

Week of October 9 • United States

A educational event sponsored by the National Fire Protection Association for more than eighty years, Fire Prevention Week is the annual tribute to fire awareness and prevention.

Holiday History *Read Aloud*

On October 8, 1871, the Great Chicago Fire burned down many homes and businesses. The fire was most likely started by a cow! Kate O'Leary's crowded barn held five cows plus hay for feed and coal and wood shavings for fuel. One of the cows probably started the fire by kicking over a lantern. The summer had been hot with little rain. The ground was dry, which helped the flames spread quickly through the city.

Fast Fact

A fire requires fuel, heat, and oxygen. The fuel can be anything that burns. The heat can come from many sources, such as a lit match, a stove, or a heater. Oxygen in the air lets the fire breathe and grow.

Fire Safety Doorknob Pull `Language Arts`

Reinforce some important rules to keep homes safe from fire with this simple craft project.

★ Review the fire safety rules below. Ask students to write the rules in capital letters on index cards and decorate with pictures of small flames with Xs through them.

★ Punch small holes in the middle of the top and bottom of the card with a hole punch or pencil.

★ Insert a shoelace down through the top hole then up through the bottom hole. Leave about 2 inches of shoelace hanging from the bottom and about 4 inches at the top.

★ Thread the bottom section of the shoelace through a small bell and knot it to secure. With the top section, make a circle large enough to fit over a doorknob, then knot it.

★ Encourage students to hang the reminder card over an important doorknob in their homes!

Fire Safety Rules

⊗ Make sure a grown-up stands next to the stove at all times when something is cooking on it.

⊗ If you see matches or lighters, don't touch them! Tell a grown-up where you found them.

⊗ Make sure portable or space heaters are at least three feet away from walls, furniture, or anything else that can burn.

⊗ Be sure that there's at least one smoke alarm on every level of your home and in or near all sleeping areas. Replace the batteries twice a year, when you turn your clocks forward and back.

⊗ Keep all the exits in your home clear of toys, trash, and clutter.

★ Book Links

No Dragons for Tea: Fire Safety for Kids (and Dragons) by Jean Pendziwol (Kids Can Press, 2001). Picture book, all ages. A friendly dragon accidentally sets the tea table on fire.

The Great Fire by Jim Murphy (Scholastic, 1995). Chapter book, intermediate. This award-winning nonfiction book about the Great Chicago Fire will fascinate older students.

~ EXCERPT ~

Make sure students practice and memorize these four steps to put out flames if their clothes catch fire:

STOP immediately where you are.

DROP to the ground.

ROLL over and over and over, covering your face and mouth with your hands (this will prevent flames from burning your face and smoke from entering your lungs). Roll over and over until the flames are extinguished.

COOL the burn with cool water for 10–15 minutes. Get help from a grown-up, and if needed, see a doctor.

—from the National Fire Protection Association Web site at **www.nfpa.org**

Halloween

October 31 • United States, United Kingdom, Canada, and other countries worldwide

Halloween is unlike any other holiday. Celebrate by sharing its vibrant history and customs, turning the fun and games into rich learning experiences.

Do some students ask not to take part in Halloween and other holiday celebrations? See Religious Holidays and Multicultural Appreciation on page 7.

Holiday History
The first Halloween celebrations in America began as public events to celebrate the harvest. Neighbors shared stories of the dead, danced, sang, and told fortunes.

In Other Words
The word *Halloween* comes from the Christian holiday All Saints' Day on November 1, which honors the saints who don't have feast days named after them. All Saints' Day was known long ago as All Hallows' Day—hallow is the Middle English word for "holy." Combined with the Scottish e'en ("evening"), it became Hallow's E'en or Holy Evening.

Trick AND Treat!   Math
Make math fun at Halloween with this game of "Trick AND Treat."
★ Each student takes a turn at trying to trick you with a very difficult math problem. (The real trick is that the student must know the answer first and have it written down.)
★ Establish rules so the game reinforces your current math lesson—without the need for a calculator.
★ If you get it right, the students get to try again! If you get the answer wrong, give a treat.

Fast Fact
Pumpkins, black cats, witches' hats . . . our favorite Halloween symbols are orange and black. These colors have their true origins in the season: Orange represents the colors of fallen leaves and the autumn harvest; black stands for the darkening sky that leads to winter. Discuss these meanings, and decorate your classroom with crafts in colors of the season.

Reproducible

Colorful Symbols of Halloween, page 42   Art
Use this reproducible to provide pictures of symbols of the season that students can hang on colorful streamers to decorate the room. FOR YOUNGER STUDENTS: Let students color in the shapes orange or black, or photocopy onto colored construction paper. FOR OLDER STUDENTS: Have students select two or more shapes to include in a spooky Halloween story. They can color and arrange the shapes on a piece of construction paper to create a cover collage for their story.

Halloween

Holiday History

The legend of the jack-o'-lantern comes from an Irish tale. According to the legend, a man named Jack played many tricks on the devil. When Jack died, his spirit was not welcome anywhere, and so his spirit roamed the countryside with only a small lantern to guide the way. Our jack-o'-lantern is a tribute to Jack and his lantern.

Fast Fact

The traditional U.S. jack-o'-lantern is made from a pumpkin. English children honor the legend of Jack by carrying small lanterns made from beets, called punkies. In Scotland, the lanterns are made from turnips and called bogies.

Around the World

British children celebrate Halloween as well as Guy Fawkes Day, which continues the ghoulishness. On November 5, 1605, Guy Fawkes tried to kill King James I in a plot to blow up the House of Parliament, the British government building. Thirty-six barrels of gunpowder were found before they exploded. The king was saved, and Fawkes was caught and hanged. Today, groups of children run up and down the streets at dark on November 5 begging for change and chanting, "A penny for the Guy! A penny for the Guy!" They hold "Guy," a straw dummy wearing clothing and a mask. In some parts of England, "Guy" is thrown into a bonfire—called a bone fire—in the town square.

Halloween Feels Like . . . `Social Studies` `Science`

Halloween takes on a creepy-crawly quality when students use their sense of touch to identify mystery foods. British favorites include:

★ Halloween worms (egg noodles)

★ witch's fingers (chicken strips)

★ eyeballs (small scoops of chocolate and vanilla ice cream)

★ witch's elixir (a mixture of fruit juices with grapes, berries, and chunks of apple and orange)

Have some spine-shivering fun: Blindfold students and ask them to touch and identify edibles such as cooked oatmeal, whipped cream, maple syrup, and chopped-up ice pops. Encourage students to use descriptive adjectives to capture the textures they feel.

★ **Book Links**

Wee Witches' Halloween by Jerry Smath (Scholastic, 2002). Picture book, easy. Fresh out of scaring school, these witches try to be scary.

Scary, Scary Halloween by Eve Bunting (Houghton Mifflin, 1988). Picture book, all ages. Cats watch trick-or-treaters.

★ **Teacher Resources**

Fresh & Fun: Halloween: Dozens of Instant and Irresistible Ideas and Activities From Creative Teachers Across the Country by Tracey West (Scholastic, 1999). For grades K–2.

Month-by-Month Poetry (September, October, and November) compiled by Marian Reiner (Scholastic, 1999). For grades PreK–2.

Fall Harvests Around the World

Did you know that the first American celebration of Halloween was a harvest festival? (See the Halloween Holiday History on page 24.) Harvest is a celebration of the bounty of crops and good food, which leads to cheerful gatherings among family and friends. Traditions of harvest festivals around the world are presented below and on page 27. Use some or all of the party ideas to hold your own international fall harvest festival.

★ Book Link

The Legend of Sleepy Hollow by Washington Irving (Penguin, 1995). Picture book, intermediate. This is the original story of Ichabod Crane and the headless horsemen with illustrations by Will Moses, the great-grandson of Grandma Moses.

Crop Over Festival ★ Barbados

This July festival originated around the harvesting of sugarcane, one of the main crops grown on this island. When the growing, cutting, and transporting were over (thus "crop over"), workers were given time to dance and feast. The festival was revived in 1974 and includes special events like sugarcane cutting contests and steel drum competitions.

★Party! Steel Drum Band ⬤ Science ⬤ Music

Bring in different sizes of food cans without their tops (make sure there are no sharp edges). With their bottom sides up, the cans become musical instruments. Let students drum with pencils to make island music. Point out to students that the more dented the can is, the higher the pitch. (Note: Before you bring the cans to class, use a hammer to dent the bottoms to create pitch variations.)

Green Corn Ceremony ★ United States/Native American

During the full moon in August or September, the busk was celebrated as the first corn harvest of the season. A holy man kindled a sacred fire symbolizing renewed life.

Loy Krathong ★ Thailand

This Thai festival celebrates water and its importance to the harvest. On the night of the full moon in mid-November, Thais meet at the river's edge and float small homemade boats illuminated with candles. Boats hold coins and nuts for good fortune in the coming year.

★Party! Loy Krathong Boats ⬤ Art

- ★ Mold a sheet of aluminum foil into the shape of a small boat.
- ★ Glue assorted decorations onto the boat.
- ★ Set a small ball of clay in the middle of the boat. Insert a birthday candle.
- ★ Suggest that students float their boats outside in a bucket of water on the evening of the next full moon. Remind them to light the candle with an adult's assistance!

Fall Harvests Around the World

Moon Festival and Tet Trung Thu ★ Hong Kong and Vietnam

Called the Mid-Autumn Festival, the Moon Festival and Tet Trung Thu are celebrated in their respective countries during the first full moon in September. It is a day to worship the harvest moon. Streets are decorated with lanterns. Children are allowed to stay up late to watch the full moon rise.

★Party! Full Moon in Focus **Science**

Paste a big white circle onto a large piece of black construction paper and hang it at the front of your classroom. Learn about the phases of the moon on the Farmers' Almanac Web site at **www.farmersalmanac.com**. Click on the Astronomy link.

N'cwala ★ Zambia, Africa

The N'cwala ceremony, held in February, is based on the Ngoni tribal tradition of offering its paramount chief the first produce of the year. Local chiefs choose their best dancers, considered to be the tribe's best warriors as well. Donning traditional costumes, they dance before the paramount chief, who selects the winning group.

★Party! Dance Contest **Music**

Let students dance to the rhythm of drums (see the Steel Drum Band activity on page 26). Students can learn a simple step or do a rhythmic task such as spinning a hoola hoop—and challenge themselves to sustain the movement! You might coordinate the event with recess or P.E. class.

Onam ★ India (Hindu)

This four-day harvest festival in September comes at the end of monsoon season. Vegetarian meals are served, often on plantain leaves instead of dishes. Parents give their children new clothes or cloth that will be made into new clothes. They sing and push each other on swings called oonjals.

★Party! Leaf Plates **Science**

For a true natural—and nutritious!—experience, serve party snacks on large edible leaves such as iceberg lettuce or kale.

Yam Festival ★ Ghana

The September harvest season is ushered in by festivities including the wearing of animal masks and the displaying of fetishes—small animal figures that give good luck to the holder. Everyone enjoys eating freshly-picked yams, a kind of sweet potato.

★Party! Harvest Foods **Science**

Munch on crunchy yams (sweet potato chips) and other natural snacks such as plantain chips, dried apples, raisins, and pumpkin seeds. Discuss how and where they grow.

The Day of the Dead

October 31, November 1 and 2 • Latin Americans worldwide/Christian

This Latin American celebration of the dead—called El Dia de los Muertos in Spanish—offers an uplifting tradition of remembrance.

★ Book Link

Day of the Dead by Tony Johnston (Harcourt, 2000). Picture book, all ages. A walk through the holiday's rituals.

The Spirit of Tio Fernando by Morella Fuenmayer (translator) (Whitman, 1995). Picture book, all ages. Nando remembers his uncle during his family's Day of the Dead preparations.

Traditions Today

According to Latin American tradition, the deceased come back to visit the living every year on this holiday. Homes feature *ofrendas*, or altars, to welcome the visiting souls. A washbasin is set by the altar so the "guests" can wash up before dining. A typical meal includes beans and sweet potatoes. Families visit the graves of loved ones, leaving colorful flowers including marigolds—the "flower of the dead." The marigold's scent is believed to attract souls back to earth.

★Talk About ★It   Why might it be important to remember and honor those who have passed away?

Fast Fact ★Read Aloud★

The skeleton is the unofficial mascot of The Day of the Dead. Traditional cakes are decorated with pieces of hardened sugar shaped and decorated to look like skulls. Children wearing skeleton costumes run through the streets yelling, *"Caleveras! Calaveras!"* (Skulls! Skulls!). People they pass give them candy, fruit, and money.

America Celebrates

Mexican Americans traditionally hold special ceremonies at home for their deceased family members. They turn in the four directions of the compass to pay tribute to these people.

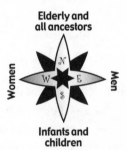

Elderly and all ancestors

Women

Men

Infants and children

Around the World

November 2 is All Souls' Day, when Europeans remember loved ones who have passed away. During the Middle Ages, on this day adults walked from door to door offering prayers for the dead. They received pastries called soul cakes in return. According to legend, whenever a soul cake was eaten, it helped release a soul into heaven. Today, Europeans have picnics at the graves of family members. After the picnic is over, all the leftovers are placed on the graves. Some people believe that the dead will eat the food later.

National American Indian Heritage Month

November 1–30 • United States

Celebrate the culture and traditions of Native Americans during the month that ends with Thanksgiving.

Holiday History *Read Aloud*

You know the stories about the past that your parents tell over and over again? They are your family's oral tradition. For Native American tribes such as the Cherokee, Iroquois, and Navajo, oral tradition is an important part of their cultural heritage. Traditionally, while the men were away hunting, the women, children, and elders—or older people—entertained themselves in the evenings by telling vivid stories around a blazing fire. The elders were the storytellers, and the children acted out the stories that were being told. This helped them become good storytellers when they grew up.

In Other Words *Read Aloud*

A tradition is a custom or a belief that is handed down from generation to generation, and oral means "spoken out loud." Oral tradition refers to the stories of the past that are handed down from one generation to another.

Traditions Today *Read Aloud*

Traditionally, members of a Native American tribe held a powwow to discuss important issues. Today, Native Americans sponsor powwows to celebrate special holidays and events. Guests are often welcome to watch history come to life as they enjoy traditional crafts, foods, and ceremonial dances. One important intertribal powwow—welcoming members of many tribes—is held each year at Trail of Tears Commemorative Park in Hopkinville, Kentucky. It attracts more than 16,000 people from all over the world. The park is a historic landmark of a tragic event in which the Cherokee people were forcibly removed from their homelands by the U.S. government. The Trail of Tears was a treacherous and deadly 1,000-mile journey from the Cherokees's homes in the Southeast to Oklahoma in 1838.

Stories of the Past `Social Studies` `Language Arts`

Invite a grandparent to come in to share a story about the past. Remember the story and share it again and again—it can become part of your class's oral tradition.

For more on Native Americans and the first Thanksgiving, see page 36.

★ **Book Links**

. . . *If You Lived With the Cherokee* by Peter and Connie Roop (Scholastic, 1998). Picture book, intermediate. This book answers many questions about the Cherokee tribes who lived in the Great Smoky Mountains in the southeastern United States from 1740 until 1838; it also includes a visit with Cherokees today. Other *If You Lived With* titles give a historic view of the Sioux, Hopi, Iroquois, and Indians of the Northwest Coast.

Children of the Earth and Sky: Five Stories about Native American Children by Stephen Krensky (Scholastic, 1991). Picture book, intermediate. These realistic fiction stories of Native American children give insight into the cultures of the Hopi, Comanche, Mohican, Navajo, and Mandan tribes.

★ **Web Link**

Wherever you live, visit the Trail of Tears by checking out **www.rosecity.net/tears**, the site of the Trail of Tears Association.

National American Indian Heritage Month

★ Book Link

Probably Pistachio by Stuart J. Murphy (HarperCollins, 2001). Picture book, all ages. The concept of probability applies to the life of a young boy who is having a difficult day. Great to use with games of probability, such as the bean game at right.

★Teacher Resources

Multicultural Discovery Activities for the Elementary Grades by Elizabeth Crosby Still (Center for Applied Research in Education, 1995).

Read aloud or act out the Apache folk tale "How Man Got Fire" from ***Folk Tale Plays From Around the World—That Kids Will Love!*** by Marci Appelbaum and Jeff Catanese (Scholastic, 2001). For grades 3–5.

Two Native American Games `Social Studies`   `Math`

1. Hit The Tree (group)

★ Tie two pieces of yarn or cloth around a tree trunk—the first should be about 2 feet up from the bottom, and the second about 15 inches above the first piece.

★ Have players stand 5 to 10 feet away from the tree (depending on their ages) and take turns throwing a soft ball at the tree. (Make sure the tree is sturdy and that the ball does not damage the bark. You might also find a different target, such as a post.) If the student hits the trunk between the pieces of yarn, he or she scores a point.

★ Make it a competition: The first player to hit the target ten times wins. Younger players might participate in teams.

2. Ancient Indian Bean Game (two players)

★ Start with a pile of ten white and ten black beans, a container, and two yellow beans (one for each player). One player tries to capture all the black beans, and the other tries to take all the white beans.

★ Players take turns. The first player places three beans (one black, one white, and his or her yellow bean) in the container, shakes it, and tosses the beans onto the ground. If the yellow bean is closer to the white bean, the white-bean player wins and keeps the white bean. The black bean is returned to the pile. If the yellow bean is closer to the black bean, the black-bean player wins and keeps the black bean, returning the white bean to the pile.

★ The first player to take all of his or her beans is the winner.

—adapted from *Multicultural Discovery Activities*

★Talk About ★It   For older students, take the opportunity to explore the concept of probability. What are the chances that a yellow bean will land closer to the black bean? To the white bean?

Mark Your Calendar

Celebrate Native American culture throughout the year.

★ American Indian Day (fourth Friday in September): Many states celebrate this holiday to honor American Indians.

★ Green Corn Ceremony (August or September): See Fall Harvest Festivals in October (page 26).

★ Sun Dance Ceremony (June or July): See Summer Solstice in June (page 115).

Election Day

Tuesday after first Monday in November • United States

On this day, U.S. citizens vote for local, county, state, and national government leaders. Provide a lesson on the importance of elections and exercising our right to vote.

Fast Fact *Read Aloud*
Why are elections so important? Our freedom depends on it! By definition, democratic nations such as the United States, Canada, and Mexico allow their citizens to elect their government leaders. Letting the people choose their leaders is an important way to make sure their voices are heard in the government. When U.S. citizens reach eighteen years of age, they can vote in elections.

In Other Words
The word *election* comes from a Latin word meaning "to choose." In an election, voters choose one person for a political office.

Vote for a Class Mascot `Social Studies`
Teach some basics about a political campaign by holding an election for classroom mascot.

★ **Take a Poll:** What does it take to make a great classroom mascot? Conduct a classroom or schoolwide poll following the activity instructions in the reproducible link below.

★ **Political Parties:** Create two or three political parties—for instance, the Stuffed Animal Party and the Class Pet Party. Introduce the concept of political parties by discussing the Democratic and Republican parties. Older students can research and compare the platforms of other parties such as the Independent and Green parties.

★ **Political Ads and Posters:** Urge students to create their own political ads to promote their favorite candidate for classroom mascot. What do these ads need to show? Explain how political advertisements on TV and in newspapers try to persuade people to vote a certain way.

★ **Election Day:** Make a special voting booth (your desk) where students choose their favorite candidate in a secret ballot. Remind them that only class citizens are allowed to vote—and that it is a special privilege. Count the votes and announce the winner!

Class Mascot Poll, page 43 `Social Studies` `Math`
Polling is the way politicians find out people's feelings and thoughts about certain issues. Take a poll to find out what makes a great classroom mascot. Ask students to vote for their favorite mascot quality by raising their hands as you call out the qualities listed on the reproducible. Each student may only respond once. Acting as pollster, calculate the percentages (number of responses divided by total students) and create a bar graph on the chalkboard using the reproducible as a guide. With this polling data, the class can choose the top two candidates for the upcoming election of classroom mascot. FOR OLDER STUDENTS: Let students calculate and graph the polling data.

★ **Web Link**
Kids Voting USA, at **www.kidsvotingusa.org**, is a student- and teacher-friendly site with activity ideas and information about a special program that enables students to visit official polling sites and "vote" on Election Day.

★ **Teacher Resource**
Candidates, Campaigns & Elections by Linda Scher and Mary Oates Johnson (Scholastic, 2000). For grades 4–8. Projects, activities, and literature links.

Reproducible

Bulletin Board Idea Re-create a large-scale bar graph of the classroom poll data. Include photos or drawings of various mascot candidates with the elected candidate displayed prominently.

Veterans Day

November 11 • United States, Canada, Australia

Discuss the history of war and the promise of peace during this holiday tribute to the fallen soldiers of World War I and all U.S. military veterans.

★ Book Link

Veterans Day: Remembering Our War Heroes by Elaine Landau (Enslow, 2002). Chapter book, intermediate. This well-written account of the holiday and of war contains engaging photographs.

★ Web Link

The Teachervision Web site at **www.teachervision.com** offers lesson plans on a variety of topics, including "The History and Poetry of 'In Flanders Fields.'"

Holiday History

Veterans Day, called Remembrance Day in Canada and Australia, honors the men and women who lost their lives while serving in war. It is celebrated on this day to commemorate the armistice that occurred on November 11, 1918, at 11 A.M. to end World War I. Today, Veterans Day in the United States honors all veterans who have served in the military.

A Moment to Reflect   Social Studies

Many people still observe one minute of silence at 11 A.M. to pay respect for the fallen soldiers and their families. Ask students to partake in one minute of silence at 11 A.M., during which time they can think about what peace means to them. Discuss their thoughts.

In Other Words

An armistice is the official suspension, or end, of fighting in order to start the process of creating a peace agreement.

★Talk About ★It — What is a peace agreement? Give an example of a peace agreement you have made with a friend or sibling.

Holiday History

John McCrae wrote his famous poem "In Flanders Fields" after a major battle in Flanders, Belgium, where he served as a surgeon with the Canadian army during World War I. His poem refers to wild poppies that began to blossom on the gravesites of soldiers in the fields. This stirring natural event provides an interesting science link: Poppy seeds can live dormant underground for years and years without growing until the soil around them is disturbed. The dormant poppy seeds in Flanders fields were given a chance to grow when the gravesites were dug.

Fast Fact ★Read Aloud★

McCrae's poem (at right) was published to help raise money for the Canadian war effort. Because of the poem's popularity, Canada adopted the poppy as the flower of remembrance. Just like we wear American flag pins on our clothing, Canadians show their patriotism by wearing poppies on their lapels on Remembrance Day.

~ In Flanders Fields ~

In Flanders fields the poppies blow
Between the crosses, row on row,
That mark our place; and in the sky
The larks, still bravely singing, fly
Scarce heard amid the guns below.

We are the Dead. Short days ago
We lived, felt dawn, saw sunset glow,
Loved, and were loved, and now we lie
In Flanders fields.

Take up our quarrel with the foe,
To you from failing hands we throw
The torch, be yours to hold it high.
If ye break faith with us who die
We shall not sleep, though poppies grow
In Flanders fields.

—Lieutenant Colonel John McCrae (1915)

Guru Nanak's Birthday

November 18 • Sikhs worldwide

Nanak was the founder of the Sikh religion in India at the end of the fifteenth century. His title was guru, or teacher. Introduce his birthday and bring about new understanding of world religions.

Fast Fact
Sikhism is a monotheistic religion that combines Hinduism and Islamic Sufism. Before Guru Nanak's birthday every year, Sikhs read his teachings: the *Guru Granth Sahib*.

In Other Words
Guru Nanak told his Hindu and Muslim followers: "There is but One God, His name is Truth . . ." The god's name is Sat Nam or "true name." People practicing yoga often repeat, "Sat Nam" to help them concentrate on breathing and meditation.

World Hello Day

November 21 • Worldwide

Say "hello" to ten people today—and start an ongoing discussion about the importance of communication between people and nations.

Holiday History
World Hello Day began in response to a conflict in the Middle East that exemplifies the importance of peaceful communication. On October 6, 1973, Egyptians attacked the Israelis to force them to surrender captured land. The day was Yom Kippur, the sacred Jewish holiday, so Israel was caught by surprise. Many lives were lost. After years of fighting, Israel and Egypt finally made peace. In November 1977, Egyptian president Anwar Sadat made a speech to Israel in Jerusalem. He was the first Arab leader ever to recognize Israel. The Sinai Peninsula, which Israel had seized in 1967, was returned to Egypt.

Traditions Today
Today, more than 180 nations participate in World Hello Day. It works because communication—even simply saying "hello" to a neighbor, friend, or stranger—reinforces the idea that we need to talk about our differences if we are to live in a peaceful world.

★Talk About ★It   How does communication help preserve world peace? Talk about it, then go out and say "hello"!

★ Book Link
Hello World! Greetings in 42 Languages Around the World by Manya Stojic (Scholastic, 2002). Picture book, all ages. Charming pictures of children teach readers how to say hello in many languages.

★ Hello! ★
English
★ Bonjour! ★
(bown-JOR) French
★ Guten Tag! ★
(GOO-ten TAHG) German
★ Ciao! ★
(Chow) Italian

Ramadan

November/date varies (29 or 30 days of the ninth month of the Muslim calendar)
• Muslims worldwide

For Muslims, the followers of Islam, Ramadan is a month of focus on spiritual goals and values. During this period, Muslims fast from sunrise to sunset.

For more about Islam and the Muslim calendar, see pages 8—9.

~ Celebrating Ramadan ~

During Ramadan, Muslims don't eat during daylight. We eat early in the morning, and after the sun has set. While my mom prepares the food, my siblings and I sneak five more minutes of sleep. Afterwards, we all eat together, which is very rare in my family. Then comes time for Fajr prayer, which is also before sunrise.

I find it a breeze to live without food for half the day. I go to Stuyvesant High School and there are many Muslim students who hang out in the prayer lobby at lunchtime.

At my old Junior High School, I had to stay in the cafeteria during lunch and I couldn't help but stare at everyone eating and stuffing themselves. But this did teach me self-restraint.

My parents' childhood was spent in Pakistan, a Muslim country. Everyone was aware about Islam and mostly everyone followed it.

When I went back to visit Pakistan, it was during Ramadan. It felt very different. People were awakened by the loud prayer announcements and no food booths were ever open during the day.

I still wonder what it feels like to grow up in that kind of environment, where no one questions your religion or beliefs.

—Tayyba, age 14, New York City, from Online NewsHour Extra at **www.pbs.org**

In Other Words

Islam is the Arabic word meaning "to submit." The Muslim people submit to the wishes of their god, Allah.

Holiday History ✳Read Aloud✳

For Muslims, Ramadan, the ninth month of their calendar year, is sacred. According to Islamic beliefs, it was during this month that the prophet Muhammad received the *Qur'an* or *Koran*, the Muslim holy book, from Allah. During Ramadan, older children and adults fast—they do not eat, drink, or take part in certain activities during daylight hours. The reason for fasting is to practice self-control, to clean the body of "overindulgence," and to have sympathy for others who might always be hungry.

✳Talk About ✳It How does missing a meal make your body feel? How might fasting be an important way to observe this holiday? On what other holidays do people fast?

Fast Fact ✳Read Aloud✳

Ramadan ends with the three-day festival of Eid-al-Fitr. Muslims first eat a light, sweet snack. Figs are a traditional snack because it is said that the prophet Muhammad enjoyed them. Then families put on holiday clothes, go to a special community prayer, and visit relatives and friends. In many places, children receive gifts. Finally, everyone enjoys a big meal.

In Other Words

As it translates from Arabic, *Eid* means joy and *Eid-al-Fitr* is a joyous festival. This holiday is also one of generosity, or al-fitr—donations to the poor.

Around the World

In Turkey, the end of Ramadan is a three-day event called *Seker Bayrami*, the Candy Holiday or Day of Sweet Things. When the men return from their holiday prayers, they are greeted with kisses and plates of sweet foods. Children receive money wrapped in fancy handkerchiefs.

National Children's Book Week

Third week in November • United States

Dedicate extra class time to children's books during this national event sponsored by the Children's Book Council.

Mark Your Calendar

Celebrate a favorite author or illustrator every month! During your read-aloud or book-talk time, or through conversations students are having about books, or as you notice what they are reading independently, key in to the authors and illustrators who capture students' interest. Work with students to collect more books by these authors or illustrators. Building classroom library collections based on student interests helps students develop great reading habits. During the month, compare and contrast collected works by a featured author or illustrator. Ask questions about the books that help students make connections between the text and their own experiences. Encourage them to respond to important story elements such as pictures, characters, events, and dialogue.

★Talk About ★It
Who is your favorite character? What does this character do that makes him or her likable or interesting? If you had to plan a vacation with this character, where would you choose to go and why? What would you do while you were there? Explain how your choices fit with this character's interests and habits.

Publishing Party `Language Arts`

Here's how to help students become published authors!

★ Devote two or three classroom hours to writing storybooks. Younger students can draw simple picture books with short, descriptive sentences; older students can write short chapter books.

★ Have students or adult volunteers type the stories. For picture books, the text should appear at the bottom of a vertical page, leaving room to paste in illustrations.

★ Include an About the Author page, featuring the child's picture and handwritten biography.

★ Buy three-hole binders with clear covers. Punch three holes in each page and secure them in the binder to create each book. Have students illustrate book covers, which can be slipped behind the clear cover.

★ Schedule a date to invite families in to listen to author readings. Helpful hint: If available, use a microphone; shy students tend to speak very softly. Enjoy some refreshments.

★ For the rest of the school year, designate a special shelf to display works by classroom authors and have students organize their books alphabetically by their last names. FOR OLDER STUDENTS: Have students order their books by genre and then alphabetically by their last names.

★ Teacher Resources

The Big Book of Picture-Book Authors and Illustrators by James Preller (Scholastic, 2001). For grades K–3. Seventy-five short and lively read-aloud biographies that introduce favorite authors and illustrators and help kids learn about the writing process. Many author biographies are also available online at **www.teacher. scholastic.com**.

Books Don't Have to be Flat by Kathy Pike and Jean Mumper (Scholastic, 1998). For grades 3–6. Innovative ways to publish students' writing with step-by-step instructions.

★ Web Link

For more ways to celebrate with books this week, check out "Celebrating Book Week A to Z" on **www.cbcbooks.org**, the Web site of the Children's Book Council. Click on Children's Book Week, then click on Celebrate.

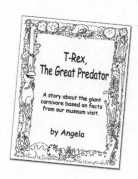

Thanksgiving

Last Thursday in November • United States (second Monday in October, Canada)

Give thanks for this holiday that teaches appreciation and respect, and also offers a lively American history lesson.

★ Book Links

Kate Waters has written many books with vivid words and pictures that take readers back in time. The re-enactment photography by Russ Kendall in the Thanksgiving books was taken at Plimoth Plantation in Massachusetts. Waters's books include:

On the Mayflower: Voyage of the Ship's Apprentice & a Passenger Girl (Scholastic, 1999). Picture book, all ages.

Giving Thanks: The 1621 Harvest Feast (Scholastic, 2001). Picture book, all ages.

Sarah Morton's Day: A Day in the Life of a Pilgrim Girl (Scholastic, 1993). Picture book, all ages.

Samuel Eaton's Day: A Day in the Life of a Pilgrim Boy (Scholastic, 1996). Picture book, all ages.

Tapenum's Day: A Wampanoag Indian Boy in Pilgrim Times (Scholastic, 1996). Picture book, all ages.

★ Teacher Resource

Primary Sources Teaching Kit: Colonial America by Karen Baicker (Scholastic, 2002). For grades 4–8. Colonial-era primary source documents, including Winslow's text (at right), the First Thanksgiving Proclamation of 1676, and a teaching guide.

Holiday History ✳Read Aloud✳

The first Thanksgiving feast was actually a traditional English harvest celebration with some special guests. It took place in what is now Plymouth, Massachusetts, in the autumn of 1621, after months of hard work and help from a nearby Native American tribe, the Wampanoag. Together they feasted on foods caught or harvested in the area, including wild turkey, which has become the most famous of Thanksgiving foods.

Fast Fact

In the 1600s, small groups of people from England began sailing to America. The Pilgrims came in 1620 so they could freely practice their own religion. Their boat, the *Mayflower*, was very small— only 90 feet long by 25 feet wide. The 102 Pilgrims, plus about 20 crew members, were crammed onto the boat for 66 days!

All Aboard! `Social Studies`

Make a class "boat" by placing several desks in a semi-circle so that there is no more than two square feet of space for each student. Invite students to board the boat. Add some stormy conditions: Produce wind by fanning magazines or phone books; create a gentle rain by spritzing the group with a plastic spray bottle filled with water.

✳Talk About ✳ It How does it feel to be "traveling" in these conditions? How might it feel for several days? Several months?

~ EXCERPT ~

Our corn did prove well, and God be praised, we had a good increase of Indian corn. . . . Many of the Indians coming amongst us, and among the rest their greatest king Massasoit, with some ninety men, whom for three days we entertained and feasted, and they went out and killed five deer, which they brought to the plantation. . . . And although it be not always so plentiful as it was at this time with us, yet by the goodness of God, we are so far from want that we often wish you partakers of our plenty.

—*Pilgrim Edward Winslow on the harvest feast of 1621*

Thanksgiving

Holiday History ✷Read Aloud✷

Although the first Thanksgiving feast took place in 1621, it wasn't until 1863 that it became a national holiday. A woman named Sarah Hale wrote letters to politicians, presenting facts about the first Thanksgiving feast and arguing the need for a day to give thanks. President Abraham Lincoln made it an official holiday, following a victory for the Union forces at Gettysburg during the Civil War.

✷Talk About It Why is it important to have a holiday dedicated to giving thanks?

Class Thanksgiving Day Activities Social Studies

Try these alternatives to a traditional "turkey and stuffing" classroom gathering. How about a Harvest Festival party? For details, see pages 26–27.

★ Popcorn Fest: Native Americans such as the Wampanoag ate plain popcorn as breakfast cereal and with soup. They threw corn kernels from the cob into the fire. The kernels popped in all directions, and then children chased them. Bring in all types of seasoned popcorn, scatter the popcorn on a clean blanket, and let students gather and munch. Note: The popcorn at the Pilgrims' Thanksgiving feast was sweetened with the sap of the sugar maple tree—so make sure to bring in some of the sweeter varieties!

★ Thanks for Our Favorite Foods: Have students bring in their favorite snacks or sweets to share with classmates. Make sure to give thanks, and then dig in!

★ Pie Contest: Ask parents to freeze a large slice of Thanksgiving pie (homemade or store-bought) and bring it in on the following Monday. Cut each piece into small bites so that students can sample and vote for their favorite.

★ "Kitty in the Corner"—a Pilgrim Game: One child playing the kitty (Pilgrims called it "puss") stands in the center of the room. The other players stand in the four corners of the room or along the walls. The object is for everyone to change places without letting the kitty get a spot. If the kitty succeeds, then the student whose spot was taken becomes the kitty for the next round.

—adapted from *Pilgrims*

★ Book Links

Thanksgiving at the Tappletons' by Eileen Spinelli (HarperCollins, 1992). Picture book, all ages. Enjoy a fun Thanksgiving with this family and compare your own family traditions to theirs.

Thanksgiving Day by Anne Rockwell (HarperCollins, 2002). Picture book, all ages. Learn the history of Thanksgiving through Charlie's school play, which explains why we eat turkey, corn bread, and cranberry sauce.

★ Teacher Resources

The Thanksgiving Activity Book: A Bountiful Collection of Ready-to-Use Activities, Games, Easy Art Projects, Poems, Mini-Books, and More by Deborah Schecter (Scholastic, 2000). For grades K–2.

Pilgrims by Susan Moger (Scholastic, 2000). For grades K–3, but many activities are appropriate for older grades. A complete theme unit developed in cooperation with Pilgrim Hall Museum.

Thanksgiving

For more Native American activities, see National American Indian Heritage Month on pages 29—30.

★ Book Links

Giving Thanks: A Native American Good Morning Message by Chief Jake Swamp (Lee & Low, 1997). Picture book, all ages. The full Native American message of Thanksgiving is provided with authentic illustrations.

Milly and the Macy's Parade by Shana Corey (Scholastic, 2002). Picture book, all ages. A young girl who is new to America experiences its traditions for the first time. The story was inspired by the first Macy's Thanksgiving Day Parade in 1924.

Around the World

Here's a look at how people in other countries give thanks.

Canada: Thanksgiving, on the second Monday of October, is a celebration of the fall harvest.

Philippines: T'Boli Tribal Festival, held during the third week in September, is a day when the people on the island of Mindanao try to recreate Lem-lunay, what they believe was a perfect society. Ten major tribes come to the city of South Cotabato to take part in traditional games and ethnic dances. The goal is to remind people that in their quest for a more perfect life, they should be thankful for what they have.

Switzerland: On September 20, villages celebrate Federal Thanksgiving Day. Cattle, adorned with flowers and tree branches, are led with cow bells ringing in a formal procession. Feasting, yodeling, and dancing to traditional music last into the night. At this time of year, local herders descend from summer pastures in the Alps.

Traditions Today

The Thanksgiving parade takes after an old ritual of celebrating the harvest season. The first parade floats were wagons in ancient Greece and Rome that were decorated with food and wheat. Today, many towns hold Thanksgiving parades. The biggest of all is the Macy's Thanksgiving Day Parade in New York City, featuring colorful floats with celebrities, marching bands, and giant balloons of popular cartoon characters.

My children take this gift.
In love do I bestow it,
And in love shall you receive it.
It will feed you and sustain you.
It will prosper you and keep you.
Through this gift of corn I bring
All your children will be blessed.
Only live in peace and friendship
with each other.

—Tuscarora poem

Thanksgiving Placemat, page 44 `Language Arts`

Let students make a special Thanksgiving dinner placemat. Read aloud the Tuscarora poem at left and discuss some of the things we are thankful for, such as friends and family, nature, and food. Distribute copies of the reproducible and invite students to write their own Thanksgiving message (or write a class poem together for students to copy). Have them color the symbols of the season around the border, cut out their finished messages, and glue the placemat copy to the center of a piece of colored construction paper. FOR OLDER STUDENTS: Many Native American cultures place a high value on their elders, the oldest people in their tribe. With this in mind, start your own Thanksgiving tradition by making special placemats for people in a local nursing home.

Reproducible

My Thanksgiving Message
by

¡Chocolate!

Chocolate Caliente
(Hot Chocolate)

★ 8 squares (8 ounces) sweetened chocolate

★ 4 cups skim milk

★ 4 drops vanilla extract

★ cinnamon

Break chocolate into small pieces. Combine chocolate, milk, and vanilla in a saucepan, constantly stirring. Bring to a boil. Use a whisk to mix it. Pour into cups. Sprinkle cinnamon on top. Serves 4—6 people.

Before drinking your chocolate caliente (pronounced choh-koh-LAH-tay kah-lee-EHN-tay), try this chant that's popular among Spanish children. As you say the numbers, count with your fingers 1, 2, 3 (uno, dos, tres). On the last line, make a stirring motion ("stir the chocolate!").

Uno, dos, tres CHO
(OOH-no, DOHS, TREHS CHOH)

Uno, dos, tres CO
(OOH-no, DOHS, TREHS KOH)

Uno, dos, tres LA
(OOH-no, DOHS, TREHS LAH)

Uno, dos, tres TE
(OOH-no, DOHS, TREHS TAY)

Bate, Bate, CHOCOLATE!
(BAH-tay BAH-tay choh-koh-LAH-tay!) (Stir the chocolate!)

Citizenship Day

Citizenship Test

The Test of Citizenship is taken by people who were born outside the United States and want to become citizens of our country. Do you know some basic facts about our country and government? Take a sample test and find out!

1. What are the three branches of government?
   A. executive, legislative, judicial
   B. executive, congressional, legal
   C. president, vice president, secretary of state

2. Which branch of the government has the offices of the president and vice president?
   A. White House
   B. executive
   C. Washington, D.C.

3. What do the stars and stripes on the United States flag represent?
   A. the past presidents of the United States
   B. the 50 states and original 13 colonies
   C. nothing—they are decorations.

4. What kind of government does the United States have?
   A. monarch
   B. congressional system
   C. democracy

5. What is the name of the president's official home?
   A. Buckingham Palace
   B. Taj Mahal
   C. the White House

6. Name a benefit of being a United States citizen.
   A. the right to vote
   B. the right to practice any religion
   C. A and B

7. What can citizens do to become informed voters?
   A. read the newspaper
   B. talk to government officials
   C. A and B

8. Where were the Declaration of Independence and the Constitution signed?
   A. New York
   B. Philadelphia
   C. Los Angeles

9. For how long do we elect a president?
   A. one year
   B. four years
   C. ten years

10. Write the Pledge of Allegiance on the back of this page or use a new page.

(Answers: See page 126.)

The Scholastic Big Book of Holidays Around the Year Scholastic Teaching Resources

Columbus Sing-Along

Sing about Columbus's voyage! These words are sung
to the tune of "My Bonnie Lies Over the Ocean."

Columbus sailed over the ocean,
Columbus sailed over the sea,
Columbus sailed over the ocean,
An eager explorer was he!

CHORUS
Sail on, sail on,
Columbus sailed over the sea, you see!
Sail on, sail on,
Columbus sailed over the sea!

In Spain, many people were laughing.
They said, "He'll fall flat off the earth!"
Columbus said, "I'll find the Indies!"
And sailed on for all he was worth!

CHORUS

Columbus soon came to an island,
With Native Americans there.
Columbus had sailed to the New World,
And so he explored everywhere!

CHORUS

Columbus did not find the Indies,
But land others found long before.
But still we remember Columbus,
Who followed his dream to explore!

CHORUS

—from *50 Thematic Songs Sung to Your Favorite Tunes*

The Scholastic Big Book of Holidays Around the Year Scholastic Teaching Resources

Halloween

Name _____

Date _____

Colorful Symbols of Halloween

Familiar colors of the season are orange and black. Which pictures should be orange? Which pictures should be black? Color and cut out the pictures.

The Scholastic Big Book of Holidays Around the Year Scholastic Teaching Resources

Name _____

Election Day

Date _____

Class Mascot Poll

Take a classroom poll: What makes a great classroom mascot? Ask your classmates to choose the quality they think is most important and tally the responses below. Use this information to find the percentage of the class voting for each quality. Then create a bar graph of your data below. Based on what you found, what kind of candidate might win an election?

A great classroom mascot must be . . .

★ Soft and cuddly: _____ out of _____ students OR _____ % of class

★ Kindhearted and fair: _____ out of _____ students OR _____ % of class

★ The biggest and toughest: _____ out of _____ students OR _____ % of class

★ The one who is always heard: _____ out of _____ students OR _____ % of class

★ Quiet and intelligent: _____ out of _____ students OR _____ % of class

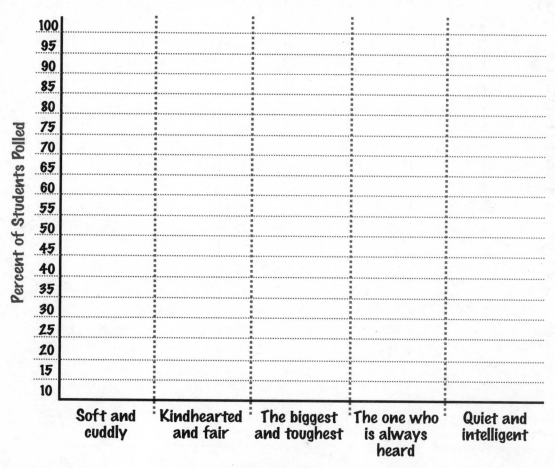

Mascot Qualities

Thanksgiving Placemat

Name _____

Date _____

My Thanksgiving Message

by _____

The Scholastic Big Book of Holidays Around the Year Scholastic Teaching Resources

(Directions, page 38)

# Winter Calendar

December

8 days in December or November	HANUKKAH	Jewish	46
December 12	DAY OF OUR LADY OF GUADALUPE	Latin America/Christian	48
December 21 or 22	WINTER SOLSTICE	Northern Hemisphere	48
December 25	CHRISTMAS	Christian	49
December 13	ST. LUCIA DAY	Sweden/Christian	52
December 16—24	LAS POSADAS	Mexico/Christian	52
December 25—January 5	WINTER FESTIVAL	Russia	53
December 26	BOXING DAY	Great Britain, Canada, Australia, South Africa	53
December 26—January 1	KWANZAA	African American	54
December 31	NEW YEAR'S EVE	Worldwide	55

January

January 1	NEW YEAR'S DAY	Worldwide	56
Third Monday in January	MARTIN LUTHER KING JR.'S BIRTHDAY	United States	57
15 days in January and/or February	CHINESE NEW YEAR	China	59
January 6	FEAST OF THE EPIPHANY	Europe/Christian	53

February

February 1—28 (or 29)	BLACK HISTORY MONTH	United States	61
February 2	GROUNDHOG DAY	United States	63
February 14	VALENTINE'S DAY	United States, other countries	64
Varies in February	100th DAY OF SCHOOL	United States	66
Third Monday in February	PRESIDENTS' DAY	United States	67
February or March	CARNIVAL	Latin America/Christian	69
February 29	LEAP YEAR DAY	Worldwide	70

 ## Winter Reproducibles

 For great ideas for celebrating students' birthdays, see Birthday Celebrations Around the World in June on pages 117—118.

Hanukkah

Eight days in December or November (eight days starting on 25th day of Kislev) • Jews worldwide

Hanukkah (also spelled Hanukah or Chanukah) is an important Jewish holiday that celebrates freedom and a miracle. Share details of this important event in Jewish history while learning about some of the holiday's more playful traditions.

> For more on Judaism and the Jewish calendar, see page 7.

★ Book Links

Alexandra's Scroll by Miriam Chaikin (Henry Holt, 2002). Picture book, intermediate. A young girl tells about life in Jerusalem in 165 B.C.

Hanukkah: A Counting Book in English, Hebrew, and Yiddish by Emily Sper (Cartwheel Books, 2001). Picture book, all ages. Students will enjoy counting in Hebrew and Yiddish with this book.

Holiday History ✦Read Aloud✦

What is the miracle of Hanukkah? More than 2,000 years ago, the Jews successfully fought to worship as they wished in the Temple. They reopened the Temple and relit the "eternal light" candle, which wasn't ever supposed to go out. Although they had enough oil for the candle to burn for only one day, a miracle occurred: The candle stayed lit for eight days until a messenger brought new oil. That's why Hanukkah lasts for eight days.

Fast Fact ✦Read Aloud✦

The menorah is the best-known symbol of Hanukkah. The special menorah of Hanukkah is called a hanukkiah. It has nine holes for candles—one for each of the eight days of Hanukkah, plus a shamesh, or "servant" candle, from which the other candles are lit.

In Other Words

Jewish children count from 1 to 8 in Hebrew for the eight days of Hanukkah. Here are the Hebrew symbols for the numbers and how they are pronounced.

1	(one)	א	(e-HAD)
2	(two)	ב	(SHTA-yeem)
3	(three)	ג	(sha-LOSH)
4	(four)	ד	(AR-bah)
5	(five)	ה	(ha-MESH)
6	(six)	ו	(SHEYSH)
7	(seven)	ז	(SHE-vah)
8	(eight)	ח	(SHMO-neh)

Count on Eight   `Math`

Form eight groups (groups can be uneven). Assign a number from 1 to 8 to each group. Let each group decorate a poster that includes the number (in English), with the Hebrew symbol and its phonetic spelling at right. Students can include the number names in other languages they know. FOR OLDER STUDENTS: Challenge students to use the Hebrew symbols in word problems they create.

Hanukkah

Holiday History *Read Aloud*

It is said that when the Syrians occupied Israel more than 2,000 years ago, they forbade children to read the Torah, the Jewish holy book. The children read it anyway. When the Syrians came to their homes, the children quickly took out their dreidels, or spinning tops, and pretended they were playing. The dreidel is now a special symbol of Hanukkah.

Talk About It Discuss how the Jewish children must have felt during the time of the occupation. How would you feel if you couldn't read a book you wanted to read or learn something that you wanted to learn?

In Other Words

The symbols or letters on dreidels today represent the first letter of each word in the Hebrew phrase "Neis gadol hayah sham," which means, "A great miracle happened here."

The Dreidel Game (Social Studies) (Language Arts)

Try this traditional spinning top game where players add to or give up their stash of goodies. Each letter or symbol on the dreidel corresponds with a move in the game:

- **נ** N (nun): The player gets nothing.
- **ג** G (gimmel): The player gets everything from the pot.
- **ה** H (heh): The player gets half the objects from the pot.
- **ש** S (shin): The player puts one object back into the pot.

How to play:

★ Pair students and give each pair a bag of goodies and a dreidel. (Though children traditionally use candy or pennies, you might include raisins or erasers.)

★ Partners take turns spinning the top. As it's spinning, children sing, "Dreidel, dreidel, dreidel, I've made you out of clay. And when you're dry and ready, then dreidel I will play."

★ Each player then takes, or gives back, the amount of goodies indicated by the dreidel symbol. The "pot" is the space or container between the players.

Homemade Dreidel (Social Studies) (Art)

Make a large dreidel: Cut a ½-gallon milk carton so that only the bottom 2 inches remain. Have students glue squares of blue paper to each side of the carton. Each square should include one letter: N, G, H, S. Poke a pencil through a hole in the bottom of the carton and then spin! To make mini-dreidels, substitute pint-sized milk cartons (rinsed out!) and follow the directions above.

Day of Our Lady of Guadalupe

December 12 • Latin America

This Latin American holiday pays tribute to Our Lady of Guadalupe, the patron saint of Mexico. To give students a glimpse of Latin American history and culture, share the famous story of her sighting on a hilltop in Mexico City nearly 500 years ago.

Holiday History

In 1532 a Mexican Indian named Juan Diego was walking on a hill in Mexico City. He claimed to have seen a vision: a young woman surrounded by a bright light who told him that she was the mother of God. Suddenly, roses appeared on the hill. The woman told Juan Diego to gather the flowers in his coat and take them to the bishop. When he opened his coat for the bishop, a painting of the woman appeared. The bishop determined that the woman was Mary, mother of Jesus. A church was built on the hill as a shrine in her honor. Today, thousands of Mexicans make the pilgrimage to the sacred hill in Mexico City to visit the shrine of Our Lady of Guadalupe.

Guadalupe Roses `Social Studies`   `Art`

Tissue paper flowers are a traditional Mexican craft. Try these simple Guadalupe roses: Cut several pieces of red tissue paper in various curved shapes and sizes. Layer them from large to small. Poke two holes about 1/2 inch apart in the center of the layers. "Sew" a pipe cleaner through the holes and then twist them to form a stem. Fluff the tissue paper petals.

Winter Solstice

December 21 or 22 • Northern hemisphere

During the first days of winter, the sun is at its lowest point in the sky, and the days have the shortest amount of sunlight. Winter solstice, celebrated as Midwinter's Day in many northern countries, is observed mostly for its historic traditions. It's a festive way for students to learn about the changing seasons.

★ Book Link

Sunshine Makes the Seasons by Franklyn M. Branley (HarperCollins, 1985). Picture book, intermediate. The importance of sunlight is made simple.

Holiday History *Read Aloud*

Throughout time, the first few days of winter were cause for celebration. People knew that following this period of limited daylight, the days would soon get longer and the sun would be bright in the sky again. The ancient Romans called this time period Saturnalia and burned lamps to get rid of darkness. Friends visited, carrying "good luck" gifts of candles and incense. People darkened their faces with paint or masks and paraded through the streets.

Changing Seasons `Science`

Take this opportunity to teach how Earth revolves around the sun, causing the seasons. The book *Sunshine Makes the Seasons* clearly demonstrates this with the help of an orange, a pencil, and a flashlight.

Traditions Today

In Nova Scotia, the winter solstice is called Children's Day. This day honors children for bringing "light" to their family's lives during these darkest days.

Christmas

December 25 • Christians worldwide

Christmas is the most important holiday for Christians around the world because it is the day that their messiah, Jesus Christ, was born. The days before winter vacation can be a time to compare and contrast the many different Christmas traditions around the world.

In Other Words

The word *Christmas* comes from Christ's Mass—the mass, or church service, for Jesus Christ.

Holiday History *Read Aloud*

Can you imagine being born anywhere besides a hospital? As told in the Bible, a very pregnant Mary and her husband, Joseph, traveled to Bethlehem. They were not able to find a room in an inn. Finally, Mary and Joseph found a stable to rest in. That's where the baby Jesus was born—on a bed of hay with animals by his side.

Advent Activity Jar, page 72 `Social Studies` `Language Arts`

A popular Christmas tradition is to follow the Advent calendar, which marks the first season of the church year and counts down from the Sunday nearest November 30 to Christmas Eve with gifts and activities. Here's a new way to count down the days to the holiday break: an Advent Activity Jar. Fill a jar with a variety of activities written on strips of paper. The reproducible page has 14 activity suggestions that you may want to photocopy, cut out, and use. You can also create your own set of advent activities, written on 3- by 5-inch index cards, cut in half lengthwise. Let students help think of quick games or tasks that the whole class can enjoy, such as lining up from shortest to tallest for the day. Each day, one or two students pick an activity. Fill a treat jar with goodies such as erasers, gummy treats, or "no homework" passes, which can serve as rewards for the completion of the activity.

Reproducible

★TIP★ Remember to plan enough time for your count-down activities to accommodate the holiday break.

Remember to be sensitive to students' diverse cultural and religious backgrounds. For information about other religious and cultural holidays during the winter season, see pages 7—9.

★ Book Links

Traditional stories of Christmas:

A Child Is Born by Margaret Wise Brown (Hyperion, 2000). Picture book, all ages. The author of ***Goodnight Moon*** writes a simple poem of the Nativity, with unique and stirring paintings by Floyd Cooper.

'Twas the Night Before Christmas: Or Account of a Visit from St. Nicholas by Clement Clarke Moore (Candlewick, 2002). Picture book, all ages. Illustrator Matt Tavares incorporates textured pencil drawings with original text from 1823, when the story first appeared in a Troy, New York, newspaper.

A Christmas Carol by Charles Dickens (HarperCollins, 2001). Picture book, intermediate. An abridged version of the famous story of Scrooge; includes audio version, teacher guide, and test questions.

Christmas

The Twelve Days ~ of Christmas ~

On the twelfth day of
Christmas, my true love
gave to me:
Twelve lords a-leaping,
Eleven ladies dancing,
Ten pipers piping,
Nine drummers drumming,
Eight maids a-milking
Seven swans a-swimming,
Six geese a-laying,
Five golden rings,
Four calling birds,
Three French hens,
Two turtle doves,
And a partridge in a pear tree.

—traditional carol

★ Book Link

The Twelve Days of Christmas
(Dodd, Mead, 1997). Picture
book, all ages. The traditional
song (complete with score) is
accompanied by Jan Brett's
illustrations in an early
American style.

★ Teacher Resource

Celebrate the Winter Holidays
by Elaine Israel (Scholastic,
2001). For grades K–2.
Activities and background
information that help kids
learn about and appreciate
five important winter holidays.

Twelve Days [Language Arts] [Math]

One favorite Christmas song is "The Twelve Days of Christmas." Let one
student be the partridge, two children be the two turtle doves, and on up
to 12 lords. Draw pictures of the 12 days and their characters so when the
student steps forward he or she can show the picture. Of course, students
may have to be several characters—which makes it a little confusing and
lots of fun! FOR YOUNGER STUDENTS: The calendar provides a great
opportunity to count backward! Hang the numbers 12 to 1 in a prominent
place to count down the days before Christmas. Each day, practice
counting backward starting with a new number. FOR OLDER STUDENTS:
What's "swans a-swimming" times "french hens"? "lords a-leaping"
divided by "turtle doves" plus "golden rings"? Older students will enjoy
this math quiz with a holiday twist.

Holiday History

A favorite symbol of Christmas is a tree decorated with ornaments and
a shining star on top. It is believed that the first Christmas tree came
from Germany during the Middle Ages. According to one legend, it was
decorated with gold and silver stars with tiny candles on the tips of the
branches. The evergreen tree is a symbol of the coming of spring, when
the earth will be green again.

Caroling Fun [Language Arts]

Sing "O Christmas Tree" to celebrate this important symbol.
You can find the full song and lyrics to dozens of other carols at
www.cameron.edu/~mikel/christmas.

Pinecone Sachet Ornament [Science]

★ Holding a pinecone at the bottom, put drops
   of glue at the tips of each level of its leaves.

★ Sprinkle one or more spices and glitter very
   lightly onto the glue.

★ Let the glue dry; hold the cone's top, turn it
   over, and do the same on the back side.

★ Thread the short end of an ornament hook through a sturdy leaf, or
   tie a piece of ribbon in a loop at the top. Hang anywhere on hooks
   or pushpins.

★ Have students try to match the scent of each pinecone to the types of
spices that were used. Encourage them to name foods that carry these
spicy scents (e.g., apple cider—cinnamon; custard—nutmeg).

—adapted from Celebrate the Winter Holidays

Christmas

Around the World

Here are some Christmas traditions from around the world.

Netherlands: On December 5, Dutch children recognize St. Nicholas Day. St. Nicholas was a fourth-century bishop who gave gifts to children. It is believed that Sinterklass (his name in Dutch) sails into the Netherlands on a big ship with a great white horse to deliver toys to good boys and girls.

Sweden: On Christmas Eve, children set out a bowl of rice porridge for Jultomten, a little elf, who arrives in a sleigh pulled by a Christmas goat.

Switzerland: In Switzerland, Weinechtchind (the Christmas Child) and six girls in rose-colored dresses visit families, sing carols, and give out cookies.

United States: Santa Claus and his sleigh led by flying reindeer bring gifts to Christian families on Christmas morning, or Christmas Eve in some homes. Santa and his elves work very hard at the North Pole to make gifts for children all over the world. He leaves presents under each family's Christmas tree.

Holiday History

How did the poinsettia become the Christmas flower? Mexicans call the flower La Flor de Nochebuena, the flower of the holy night. For hundreds of years, Mexicans have adorned their churches and nativity scenes at Christmas with the poinsettia's brilliant red leaves. Joel Roberto Poinsett, who served as the U.S. ambassador to Mexico after Mexico's independence from Spain in the early 1800s, became the flower's biggest fan. He would admire them so much upon his visits to Mexico that one Christmas he brought flowers to decorate his home in Charlestonville, South Carolina. The next year, his whole town was abloom with the Mexican flower. He spent the last years of his life promoting the poinsettia as the Mexican symbol of Christmas throughout the world.

December Match-Up, page 71 `Social Studies` `Language Arts`

December is holiday month! December events are educational and enriching for students, no matter what their religion or culture. Let students have some fun learning about December holidays with this holiday symbol–word match. FOR YOUNGER STUDENTS: Talk about the holiday symbols. Write their names, discuss their meanings and importance, and let students color the pictures.

Reproducible

★ Book Links

Writer and illustrator **Tomie dePaola** specializes in retelling cultural tales. His books include:

Merry Christmas, Strega Nona (Harcourt, 1991). Picture book, all ages. This charming Italian tale focuses on a beloved dePaola character, Grandmother Witch.

The Legend of the Poinsettia (Putnam, 1997). Picture book, all ages. This Mexican folk tale tells the story of a little girl's precious gift to the Christ child.

An Early American Christmas (Holiday House, 1991). Picture book, all ages. A German family in colonial New England is not allowed to celebrate Christmas.

Students will love untraditional Santa Stories such as:

The Polar Express by Chris van Allsburg (Houghton Mifflin, 1985). Picture book, all ages. A train ride to the North Pole features captivating illustrations.

Olive, the Other Reindeer by J. Otto Siebold and Vivian Walsh (Chronicle, 1997). Picture book, all ages. Olive the dog thinks she's a reindeer—then she saves Christmas.

A New, Improved Santa by Patricia Rae Wolff (Scholastic, 2002). Picture book, all ages. Santa has some New Year's resolutions. But do kids really want a slimmer, hipper, cyber-Santa?

★ Teacher Resource

Christmas Around the World by Mary D. Lankford (William Morrow, 1995). This thorough and engaging book features Christmas traditions from many countries.

Holidays of the Christmas Season Around the World

Reading about these special holidays during the Christmas season will help students understand many cultures and enjoy new traditions.

St. Lucia Day ★ Scandinavia/Christian ★ December 13

This holiday celebrates the life of an Italian girl who was killed in the fourth century because of her religious beliefs. Lucia, born into a wealthy Sicilian family, dedicated her life to Christianity. She carried food to Christians living in dark underground tunnels. To light her way, Lucia wore a crown of candles on her head. When she refused to marry, her angry suitor had her sentenced to death. Lucia is a patron saint in Italy, but Scandinavians also treasure her story and celebrate the holiday. As the tradition goes, the eldest daughter of a family (the "Lucia bride") puts on a white dress with a red sash and a crown of candles. The other girls wear white dresses and halos, and the boys ("star boys") wear long white shirts and pointed hats. The Lucia bride wakes the family with a special song, and then serves the family breakfast.

In Other Words

This feast day is the shortest day of the year in Scandinavian countries. In Swedish, lucia means "light"—and it is believed that the saint brings the sunshine for longer days to come.

Lucia Cats Social Studies

Make some traditional Swedish lussekatter, or "Lucia cats": Use ready-to-bake cinnamon rolls with two big raisins or chocolate chips for eyes.

Las Posadas ★ Mexicans worldwide/Christian ★ December 16–24

This Mexican holiday (pronounced LAHS poh-SAH-dahs) is celebrated with a re-enactment of Mary and Joseph's search for lodging in Bethlehem on the night of Jesus's birth. (*Posadas* is the Spanish word for "inn.") During the nine days before Christmas, groups of children carrying candles travel from house to house in their neighborhoods. People at each house tell them that "there is no room at the inn," until finally they are invited into a home or church holding a festive party.

Piñata Break Science

Every Las Posadas party features a piñata. Hang up a piñata in your classroom (the papier-mâché kind can be made or purchased in any party store) and test the best tools for breaking the piñata. Display a variety of safe objects such as a sponge, a flexible ruler, a paperback book, a rubber ball. Ask students to evaluate the object: What is it made of? How much does it weigh? How could you use the object to break open the piñata? Take the activity outside and supervise students as they use the objects to break open the piñata. Discuss which tool was most effective and why. Then let students enjoy the candy bounty!

America Celebrates

In San Antonio, Texas, people celebrate Las Posadas with a procession of boats sailing down the river that runs through the center of the city. A couple representing Mary and Joseph sits in the first boat. Other boats are filled with people singing.

Holidays of the Christmas Season Around the World

Winter Festival ★ Russia ★ December 25—January 5

Although Christmas is not officially recognized in Russia, this 12-day festival is similar to the Christian holiday. On New Year's Day, Grandfather Frost, or Dyed Maroz, delivers presents. Russians decorate evergreen trees, called New Year's trees.

In Other Words

Russian nesting dolls are called matryoshka dolls—matryoshka means "grand-mother." The traditional dolls look like Russian grandmothers wearing babushka scarves over their heads. They are given as Winter Festival gifts.

Winter Nesting Boxes Social Studies

For a fun craft, bring in lidded boxes of all shapes and sizes that can nest together (jewelry boxes up to shoeboxes). Have the class think of clues and symbols that represent winter—weather, seasonal games, holidays, songs, crafts, and so forth. Divide class into groups and let each group of students choose a clue to work with and a box to decorate. They can include a clue message in each box. When the boxes are finished, nest them and set the nesting boxes in a place for visitors to enjoy.

Boxing Day ★ Great Britain, Canada, Australia, South Africa ★ December 26

Boxing Day is the day to give tip money to people who provide important services all year long—like mail carriers, garbage collectors, and babysitters. In South Africa, it's appropriately called the Day of Good Will. This holiday may have originated long ago when service people received boxes of gifts from those they served. These gifts were given to them on the day after Christmas.

Box-a-Thank You Social Studies

Before the winter break begins, invite students to make small gifts and cards for those people who help make the school day run smoothly. Let students decorate small boxes with paint, wrapping paper, aluminum foil, ribbon, and other craft items. Fill the boxes with chocolate coins and other handmade "tips" and give them as gifts to the school nurse, secretary, custodian, librarian, lunch helpers, and other school staff. Include cards describing what students have learned about Boxing Day.

Feast of the Epiphany/Three Kings' Day ★ Europe/Christian ★ January 6

While some European children do get gifts under the tree at Christmas, many more gifts are given on the Feast of the Epiphany. Also called Three Kings' Day, the holiday honors Balthazar, Melchior, and Gaspar, the three kings (or wise men) who visited Mary and Joseph upon the birth of Jesus. They brought gifts of gold, frankincense, and myrrh with them. Today, children leave their shoes under the Christmas tree, and small gifts are left inside the shoes. When children are naughty, they expect the three kings to leave coal—but it's coal made of sugar, which is good enough to eat.

Shoe Surprise Social Studies

Ask each student to bring in a shoe and leave it by his or her desk at the end of the school day on or around January 5. (You might want to bring in several extra shoes from your own collection.) Place special treats, crafts, or school supplies in the shoes to surprise students in the morning.

Kwanzaa

December 26–January 1 • United States

Kwanzaa is celebrated by many African-American families in the United States. Each day of Kwanzaa is dedicated to one of seven principles: unity, self-determination, collective work and responsibility, cooperative economics, purpose, creativity, and faith. These principles make an excellent springboard for discussing values and traditions.

In Other Words

Kwanzaa comes from the phrase matunda ya kwanz, which means "first fruits" in Swahili, a language widely spoken in Africa. The first fruits refer to the first crops of Africa's harvest, which occurs at this time.

Holiday History *Read Aloud*

Though Kwanzaa was first celebrated in 1966, this holiday has roots in the first-fruits celebrations of ancient African civilizations such as Egypt and Nubia. The holiday's founder was Dr. Maulana Ron Karenga, a professor at the University of California at Los Angeles, who was originally from Nigeria, Africa. He believed that African Americans needed a holiday to keep them in touch with African culture and to remember the fight for their rights in this country.

Fast Fact

The colors on the African Liberation flag are symbolic for African Americans:

BLACK is for the people and their unity.
RED is for their struggle.
GREEN is for the motherland Africa and hope for the future.

These colors are important during Kwanzaa. The kinara, the special candle-holder of Kwanzaa, has seven candles: three red candles, one black candle, and three green candles. On each day of the holiday, one candle is lit.

Traditions Today

The Kwanzaa tradition says that if children make promises and keep them during the year, they are rewarded with handmade gifts called zawadi.

Zawadi Jewelry Social Studies

Make some simple jewelry in the colors of Kwanzaa with shoelaces and decorative craft items you can string on the laces.

★ Paint pieces of uncooked tube- or shell-shaped pasta. Sprinkle the pasta with glitter if desired.

★ Place the pasta on wax paper to dry.

★ Lace shoelaces through the pasta, beads, and buttons.

★ Drape around the neck and tie the ends to create a necklace.

For more celebrations of African-American culture, see:
★ Martin Luther King Jr.'s Birthday in January on pages 57–58.
★ Black History Month in February on pages 61–62.

★ Book Links

My First Kwanzaa Book by Deborah M. Newton Chocolate (Scholastic, 1992). Picture book, all ages. Readers walk through the traditions of each day of Kwanzaa.

The Seven Days of Kwanzaa: How to Celebrate Them by Angela Shelf Medearis (Scholastic, 1994). Chapter book, intermediate. A complete look at the holiday, with many craft activities—including making your own mkeka mat, a traditional straw mat of Kwanzaa.

★ Teacher Resource

For more about the history, culture, practices, and symbols of Kwanzaa, see www.Official KwanzaaWebsite.org.

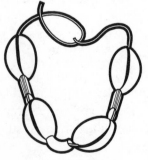

New Year's Eve

December 31 • Worldwide

New Year's Eve, the evening before the first day of the New Year, is filled with celebration and promise. Although school is closed on this national holiday, students will benefit from its message when they return to begin a new term.

America Celebrates

On New Year's Eve, Americans traditionally get together at night with family or friends. At ten seconds to midnight, they begin counting down to the new year. At the stroke of midnight, they blow noisemakers, kiss, exchange "Happy New Year" greetings, and sing "Auld Lang Syne."

★Talk About It   Auld lang syne is Scottish for "old long ago." Why is "old long ago" important on this first day of the new year?

Fast Fact ★Read Aloud★

Everyone around the world shouts "Happy New Year" at midnight on January 1—but not at the same time! Where you live determines when midnight will occur. That's because Earth has 24 time zones, based on its 24-hour rotation period. Each time zone is marked on maps by lines of longitude or meridians. Most of the United States is divided into four time zones: eastern, central, mountain, and pacific. When you go from one time zone to the next, east to west, it's an hour earlier. So when people in New York celebrate the new year, people in Los Angeles still have to wait three hours for midnight!

> ### ~ Auld Lang Syne ~
>
> Should auld acquaintance be forgot,
> And never brought to mind?
> Should auld acquaintance be forgot,
> And auld lang syne?
>
> Chorus:
> For auld lang syne, my dear,
> For auld lang syne.
> We'll tak' a cup o' kindness yet,
> For auld lang syne.
>
> —Robert Burns (1796)

Around the World

Here are some New Year's Eve traditions from other countries.

Brazil: New Year's Eve is also the ancient ritual of Lemanja, a celebration of the sea. People dress in white and gather on Brazilian beaches. Candles in the sand form beautiful, symbolic patterns. They burn brightly while offerings of flowers and food float out to sea. Brazilians then dance and sing into the night.

Denmark: New Year's Eve is a night of pranks. Young people ring doorbells in their neighborhoods and then run. At the end of the evening, the children are caught and brought indoors for treats.

Great Britain (Scotland): The first visitors of the New Year are important in many countries. In Great Britain, the "first footers" are the first people to pass through the doorway during the New Year. They arrive with gifts and food. In Scotland, during Hogmanay, the first visitors bring bread, salt, and coal. Throughout the evening, people dance the Scottish reel to songs played on bagpipes.

Netherlands: The Dutch set bonfires in the streets and enjoy elaborate fireworks displays.

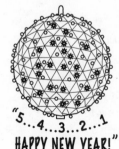

"5...4...3...2...1
HAPPY NEW YEAR!"

Traditions Today

One of the biggest and most famous New Year's Eve parties is at Times Square at 42nd Street in New York City. Thousands of people crowd together there to watch a large crystal ball descend from a flagpole atop One Times Square at midnight. People all over the world watch this event on television.

New Year's Day

January 1 • Worldwide

New Year's Day is the international holiday celebrating the first day of the new year. It's worth revisiting this holiday the day after winter vacation to enjoy New Year's traditions and explore the meaning of "starting new."

New Year's Day marks the first day of the Gregorian calendar. To learn more about the Gregorian calendar, see Leap Year Day on page 70.

Around the World

Here are some fun January 1 traditions from around the world.

Canada: Canadians, like Americans, sleep late and relax. Families may watch hockey or football on TV or enjoy outdoor sports such as skiing.

Ecuador: In Ecuador, parades through the center of towns feature a giant puppet character wrapped in cloth. It is set on fire to symbolize that all problems from the previous year will go up in smoke.

France: During France's celebration called Peille Fête, children write letters to their mothers apologizing for the things they did wrong in the previous year.

Fast Fact

Before our current calendar was invented, the New Year used to begin on April 1. (To find out why, see April Fool's Day on page 88.)

Traditions Today

While many cities hold New Year's Day parades, Philadelphia hosts the most famous of them all—the Mummers Parade. The mummers tradition dates back to the Roman festival of Saturnalia (see Winter Solstice, December 21 or 22, on page 48) where masked people played jokes on each other and made noise to scare off demons. About 30,000 "mummers" march in elaborate costumes and blow noisemakers.

America Celebrates

Americans traditionally make a list of New Year's resolutions—promises to themselves for the coming year. Popular resolutions for children might include doing better in school and listening to their parents.

★Talk About ★It
Why do people make resolutions? Why are goals important?

New Year's Resolutions, page 73 (Language Arts) ★Reproducible★

Distribute copies of this reproducible and have students keep a log of resolutions they, their families, and their friends have made. Students can make resolutions to accomplish important goals in the classroom over the month ahead. Consider having the class set a goal together. Encourage students to select a goal with anticipated results that they can easily keep track of, such as reading a chapter book each week.

★Bulletin Board ★Idea
Results that produce numbers can be graphed each week to reinforce math skills. Posting the resolutions and displaying the results prominently will motivate all of you!

Mark Your Calendar

New Year's resolutions are for teachers, too! Here's one: Start a journal project to last until the end of the school year with e-pen pals. Partner your students up with pen pals in another state or country through a program such as e–Pals at **www.EPALS.com**. Have students journal their weekly e-mail exchanges and share the new information they've learned with the class. What is their pen pal's school like? What is their pen pal's favorite subject? What does he or she do for fun? Younger students will need help from home with writing letters and journaling. (Students who do not have access to e-mail can mail letters or postcards.)

Martin Luther King Jr.'s Birthday

Third Monday in January • United States

The stories of Martin Luther King Jr.'s life and dream provide essential lessons about civil rights and peaceful conflict resolution for all students.

Holiday History ⋆Read Aloud⋆

Dr. Martin Luther King Jr. was born on January 15, 1929, in Alabama. He was one of the leaders of the civil rights movement in this country. In his short life, King helped earn many rights for African Americans. In 1968, he was shot and killed on the balcony of his hotel room. In 1983, King's birthday became a national holiday.

In Other Words

Martin Luther King's real name was Michael. His father changed it to Martin Luther (M.L. for short) after the sixteenth-century religious reformer. He wanted his son to follow in Martin Luther's footsteps.

⋆Talk About It⋆ How was Martin Luther King Jr. a reformer (someone who works to change something that is wrong or unjust)? King advocated nonviolent solutions, such as sit-ins and protests, to the problems of inequality and violence against African Americans. Why do you think he wanted to solve these problems this way?

> For more celebrations of African-American culture, see Black History Month in February on pages 61–62.

★ Book Links

Happy Birthday, Martin Luther King by Jean Marzollo (Scholastic, 1993). Picture book, all ages. The story of King told with inspirational pictures.

I Have a Dream by Dr. Martin Luther King Jr. (Scholastic, 1997). Picture book, intermediate. Dr. King's famous speech, illustrated by fifteen award-winning children's book artists.

Fast Fact

Before the Civil Rights movement, African Americans were segregated from white society in many places throughout the United States. Unfair laws and racist traditions forced them to attend different schools, sit in different seats on buses, and even drink from different water fountains. King devoted his life to ending segregation.

~ EXCERPT ~

I have a dream that my four little children will one day live in a nation where they will not be judged by the color of their skin but by the content of their character.

—Martin Luther King Jr.
"I Have a Dream" speech

Fast Fact ⋆Read Aloud⋆

Martin Luther King Jr. led citizens in many protest marches in the 1960s. During a protest, people speak up for something important; civil rights protesters called for equal rights for African Americans. At the March on Washington, D.C., on August 28, 1963—the largest civil rights protest in history to that point—marchers protested unfair employment practices that denied jobs to blacks. King gave a famous speech called "I Have a Dream." Its words still inspire hope today.

Martin Luther King Jr.'s Birthday

★ Teacher Resources

Primary Sources Teaching Kit: Civil Rights by Karen Baicker (Scholastic, 2002). For grades 4–8. Reproducible authentic documents from the era of the civil rights movement, including posters, speeches, photographs, legal papers, political cartoons and more. Includes a chapter on King's March on Washington, excerpts from his "I Have a Dream" speech, and the sheet music for "We Shall Overcome."

Read, Sing, and Learn Mini-Books: Famous Americans by Rose Crocco and Agnes Dunn (Scholastic, 2002). For grades 2–4. Twenty reproducible books with mini-biographies, fun facts, activities, and super songs set to familiar tunes. Includes a mini-book on King.

Alike and Different, page 74 `Social Studies`

Reinforce King's belief that people can be different and yet work together for the common good. This reproducible asks students to identify differences and similarities among people. FOR YOUNGER STUDENTS: Pair students and ask them to find out more about each other. Let them draw pictures of how they are different and alike.

Fast Fact

"We Shall Overcome" is the unofficial anthem of the fight for civil rights around the world. The verse, taken from Charles Tindley's gospel song "I Shall Overcome" written in 1900, was first sung during a strike by workers of the Negro Food and Tobacco Union in Charlestown, South Carolina, in 1945.

Reproducible

~ EXCERPT ~

We shall overcome,

We shall overcome,

We shall overcome some day,

Chorus:

Oh, deep in my heart I do believe

We shall overcome some day.

—adaptation by Zilphia Horton, Frank Hamilton, Guy Carawan, and Pete Seeger

Fast Fact

In 1965, Martin Luther King decided to draw public attention to a major injustice: unequal voting rights in the South. At that time, very few blacks could exercise their rights as U.S. citizens to vote because white officials often used intimidation and unfair practices, such as administering tests, when registering black voters. King organized a protest march in Selma, Alabama, where protesters walked to the local courthouse to voice their complaints about the current system. When the protesters did not make any progress, King decided to lead a march to the state legislature. Police used tear gas and clubs to break up the march, which was shown on television and shocked the nation. Undeterred, King led a second Selma-to-Montgomery march, which was a huge success. The protest gained strength, growing from 4,000 marchers to more than 25,000. It made news around the country and caused President Johnson to ask for a bill that would eliminate discriminatory practices in voter registration in the South. This bill became the Voting Rights Act of 1965.

★Talk About ★It What is a protest? How did this protest help support voting rights for black people in 1965? How might you protest something you feel is unfair?

Chinese New Year

15 days in January and/or February (15 days starting the first day of the Chinese Calendar)
• Chinese worldwide

The Chinese New Year is the most important festival of the year in China and for many Chinese around the world. Learning about the captivating traditions of this 15-day festival gives students a flavor of Chinese culture.

Fast Fact
What's the date of the Chinese New Year? Look up in the sky. The Chinese New Year starts at the second new moon after the beginning of winter in the northern hemisphere—which is some time in January or February. (For more on the Chinese lunar calendar, see Kite Festival in September on page 13.)

Holiday History *Read Aloud*
The legend behind Chinese New Year is about a dragon called Nian, which means "year" in Chinese. Nian attacked a village at the end of every winter. When the winter moon came, the villagers hid inside their homes because they knew Nian would return. But one year, the villagers built a bonfire. The fire's red light and its crackle and hiss scared away the dragon. That's why people hang red signs, blow noisemakers, and set off firecrackers on this holiday.

Fast Fact *Read Aloud*
The Chinese New Year parade is best known for the Dragon Dance, performed by dancers who move under a giant paper or silk dragon puppet stretched over bamboo poles. The dragon symbolizes long life and prosperity. Many dancers are needed to carry the dragon puppet, which can be more than 50 feet long! The dragon dancers twist and turn the puppet to chase a yellow globe that represents the sun. It is said that if the dragon catches the sun, the sun will go out. Of course, the dragon never catches it!

Dragon Tag `Social Studies`
Play this Chinese game in which students become the dancing dragon!

★ Have players line up to form the dragon. The first person in line is the dragon's head, the last person is its tail. To connect the head, tail, and body, each player should place his or her hands on the shoulders of the player directly in front.

★ To start the game, the tail player shouts out, "3, 2, 1 dragon!" With the head player leading and everyone else holding on, the dragon starts to walk quickly—twisting and turning, trying to catch its tail. As the head player darts after the tail player, all players must be careful not to let the body break (not to have any student's hands let go of the shoulders in front of him or her).

★ If its body breaks, the turn is over, and the head player moves to the end of the line to become the tail. The next player in line becomes the new head.

★ One point is scored each time the head player tags the tail player. The player with the most points wins.

—adapted from *The Multicultural Game Book*

★ Book Link
The Dancing Dragon by Marcia Vaughan (Mondo Publishing, 1996). Picture book, easy. A simple poem explains the rituals of the Chinese New Year parade. The book unfolds to reveal a long and colorful dragon.

★ Teacher Resource
The Multicultural Game Book by Louise Orlando (Scholastic, 1993). For grades 1–6. More than 70 traditional games from 30 countries.

Chinese New Year

Chinese New Year Festival   `Social Studies`

Enjoy some traditions of Chinese New Year with students. Prepare for a festival by doing some of these activities the day before.

★ Good Luck Banners

Chinese families decorate their doors with banners that have good luck phrases written in gold ink. Have students draw one of the following lucky phrases on a piece of red construction paper with a gold-colored marker or crayon:

Fooh! (May you have happiness and great fortune!)
Huang-chin wan-liang! (May you have ten thousand pieces of gold!)
Gung hay fat choy! (Prosperous and happy new year!)

★ Lantern Festival

On the fifteenth and final day of the celebration, the famous Lantern Festival is held. Thousands of lanterns in the shapes of important Chinese symbols hang in the streets, lighting up the night sky. Make your own lanterns with a string of multicolored Christmas lights. Have students cut out birds, fish, stars, and other important symbols from heat-resistant paper (see Chinese zodiac on page 95). Tape each shape over a light and hang the lights around your classroom door.

★ "Lucky Money"

A traditional Chinese New Year gift to children is "lucky money"—a red envelope with a few coins inside. The day before your celebration, have each student make a design and write their own good luck message on a white envelope with a red marker or crayon. After class, you can fill envelopes with a few pennies for the next day's festivities.

★ Festival Snacks

Share favorite New Year's snacks like dumplings, almond cookies, chestnuts, and tangerines (which symbolize good luck).

★ Tet Tradition

Vietnam calls its New Year celebration Tet Nguyen Dan ("first day" in Vietnamese). During this seven-day festival, people return to their former schools to visit and honor their past teachers. Let students take turns visiting their teachers from previous years and giving them special cards and Chinese New Year snacks.

Black History Month

February 1–28 (or 29) • United States

February is the month when schools officially celebrate African-American history and culture. It coincides with the birthdays of famous ex-slave, abolitionist, and educator Frederick Douglass (February 14) and President Abraham Lincoln (February 12).

Holiday History

The United States has celebrated Black History Month (originally Negro History Week) since 1926. Carter G. Woodson was a child of former slaves who spent his childhood working in Kentucky mines. Enrolling in high school at age twenty, he went on to earn his Ph.D. from Harvard University. Woodson dedicated his life to writing about great black Americans in history at a time when very little information was recorded or studied. He established this holiday to bring attention to the achievements of African Americans.

For more about Abraham Lincoln, see Presidents' Day in February on pages 67–68. For more about civil rights leader Martin Luther King Jr., see Martin Luther King's Birthday in January on pages 57–58.

~ I, Too, Sing America ~

I am the darker brother.
They send me to eat in the kitchen
When company comes,
But I laugh,
And eat well,
And grow strong.

Tomorrow,
I'll be at the table
When company comes.
Nobody'll dare
Say to me,
"Eat in the kitchen,"
Then.

Besides,
They'll see how beautiful I am
And be ashamed——

I, too, am America.

—Langston Hughes (1925)

Fast Fact

Langston Hughes was born in Joplin, Missouri, in 1902. Influenced by jazz and blues music, he left college, where he had been studying engineering, and began to write. Hughes emerged as a talented writer who wrote proudly about his identity as a black person. In 1925 he wrote one of his most famous poems, "I, Too, Sing America," (at left) after being turned down for a job on a ship because of the color of his skin.

★Talk About ★It
What is Langston Hughes feeling? What does he mean when he writes, "I, too, am America"?

Mark Your Calendar

For the theme of this year's Black History Month, contact the Association for the Study of African-American Life and History (ASALH) at **www.asalh.com**. ASALH sells Black History Month publications and study kits.

★ Teacher Resource

African Americans Who Made a Difference: 15 Plays for the Classroom (Scholastic, 1997). For grades 4–8. These riveting read-aloud plays tell the stories of 15 inspiring African-Americans: Rosa Parks, Jackie Robinson, Harriet Tubman, Martin Luther King Jr., Langston Hughes, and more. Plays can be read aloud to younger students.

Black History Month

★ Book Links

Extraordinary African-Americans by Susan Altman (Scholastic, 2001). Chapter book, intermediate. Biographical information on African Americans appears in this book.

Scholastic's ***African-American Collection***. A collection of 20 books on African Americans for grades 4–6 is available at a significant discount from Scholastic's Collections catalog (page 53, item CCD14893).

African-American Hero Collector Cards, page 75 `Social Studies` `Language Arts`

How have African Americans changed the world? Let each student select the name of an African-American hero (see list below for ideas) to research at home or with school resources. The reproducible page includes a collector card format that invites students to record and share what they've learned. FOR YOUNGER STUDENTS: Read about one African American, and fill in the reproducible card as a class. Ask students to draw a picture of the person's greatest accomplishment in the frame.

Reproducible

★Bulletin Board ★Idea The cards can be posted or placed along a wall-length timeline for an engaging bulletin board display.

Here is a brief list of some famous African Americans whom students can select for their African-American Hero Collector Cards or for a class timeline.

- ★ Dred Scott, plaintiff in slave lawsuit (1795–1858)
- ★ Sojourner Truth, women's rights activist (1797–1883)
- ★ Harriet Tubman, Underground Railroad conductor (1821–1913)
- ★ Booker T. Washington, educator (1856–1915)
- ★ George Washington Carver, scientist (1861–1943)
- ★ Ida B. Wells-Barnett, journalist (1862–1931)
- ★ Scott Joplin, pianist/composer (1868–1917)
- ★ W.E.B. Du Bois, civil rights leader (1868–1963)
- ★ Bessie Smith, blues singer (1894–1937)
- ★ Elizabeth "Bessie" Coleman, pilot (1896–1926)
- ★ Paul Robeson, actor and singer (1898–1976)
- ★ Marian Anderson, opera singer (1897–1993)
- ★ Edward "Duke" Ellington, jazz musician and composer (1899–1974)
- ★ Langston Hughes, writer (1902–1967)
- ★ Thurgood Marshall, Supreme Court justice (1908–1993)

- ★ Jesse Owens, track and field Olympic medalist (1913–1980)
- ★ Rosa Parks, civil rights activist (1913–)
- ★ Billie Holiday, jazz singer (1915–1959)
- ★ Jackie Robinson, baseball player (1919–1972)
- ★ Malcolm X, black power leader (1925–1965)
- ★ Medgar Evers, civil rights leader (1925–1963)
- ★ Martin Luther King Jr., civil rights leader (1929–1968)
- ★ Maya Angelou, poet (1928–)
- ★ Alvin Ailey, dancer/choreographer (1931-1989)
- ★ Henry "Hank" Aaron, baseball player (1934–)
- ★ Colin Powell, Secretary of State (1937–)
- ★ Marian Wright Edelman, children's advocate (1939–)
- ★ Muhammad Ali, boxer (1942–)
- ★ Mae C. Jemison, astronaut (1956–)
- ★ Tiger Woods, golfer (1975–)

Groundhog Day

February 2 • United States and Canada

On this quirky holiday, the groundhog is our gauge to tell us if spring is nearly here. Students will love the mascot, and you can weave in a quick lesson about weather and tradition.

Holiday History

Since ancient Rome, Candlemas Day on February 2 was designated to predict the coming of spring. People believed that "If Candlemas Day is fair and clear, there'll be two winters in the year"—meaning it would stay colder for much longer that year. In Germany, Austria, and countries across northern Europe, people watched to see if hibernating animals came out of their nests. This tradition came to America with European colonists. The German colonists in Pennsylvania watched the groundhog because it is one of the more common hibernating animals there.

Fast Fact *Read Aloud*

On February 2, it is said that the groundhog comes out of its hole after hibernating all winter to see if spring is approaching. The theory is that if it sees its shadow, which means the sun is shining, there are six weeks left of winter. The groundhog returns to its hole. If it's cloudy or rainy, there is no shadow. The groundhog takes this as a sign of the approach of spring and doesn't return to its hole.

America Celebrates

The groundhog Punxsutawney Phil from Punxsutawney, Pennsylvania, is the official groundhog of Groundhog Day. People from all over the country wait each year to see if he sees his shadow.

The Groundhog's Shadow   `Science`

Teach students about shadows. Ask students to choose their own "groundhogs" (a stuffed animal from home or any school object). Find a sunny area on concrete or the ground where shadows will appear. Explain that a shadow is formed when an opaque object—something that's not clear—blocks light. (If a student is having trouble seeing the shadow for his or her object, choose a tall stationary object such as a tree or flagpole.) In the morning, the sun is in the east, so the shadow should be on the west side of the groundhogs. Have students observe the direction and length of the shadow throughout the day. In the middle of the day (before lunch), the sun is highest in the sky so the shadow should be shortest. Late in the day, the shadow should be to the east of the groundhog since the sun sets in the west.

*Bulletin Board *Idea Let students draw pictures of their groundhogs for the bulletin board. Have them chart their shadow activity findings at various times of the day. Chart categories can include: time, location, shadow's height, width, and direction (north, south, east, west).

TIP Students can make their own compasses on a piece of paper, which they can adjust to show which direction they are facing and set on the ground for reference. Help them use the position of the sun to orient themselves. Keep an actual compass on hand to check for accuracy. Also, bring out rulers, yard sticks, or measuring tape to measure and record the length of the shadows. Select a sunny day—which might not be February 2!—to assure a successful project.

★ **Web Link**

Check out **www.groundhog.org** for lots of fun groundhog lore from the Punxsutawney Groundhog Club. Students can see Phil's predictions dating back to 1887!

Valentine's Day

February 14 • United States and other countries

Be mine! Valentine's Day is a day for exchanging notes that say you care—and teaching about what caring really means.

★ Teacher Resources

Fresh & Fun Valentine's Day by Joan Novelli (Scholastic, 1999). For grades K–2. Dozens of instant and irresistible ideas and activities from creative teachers across the country.

The Kids Care Book by Joan Novelli and Beth Chayet (Scholastic, 1991). For grades 1–6. Fifty class projects that help kids help others.

Give someone a compliment about something he or she did well today.

Holiday History

Valentine's Day was named after Saint Valentine. As one legend goes, Valentine was arrested and sentenced to death for helping Christians escape from cruel Roman prisons. While in jail, he fell in love with the jailor's daughter. Before Valentine was killed on February 14, he wrote a loving note to the girl and signed it "from your Valentine." Valentine's Day first became popular in the United States during the Civil War when soldiers sent valentines to their sweethearts from faraway camps and battlefields.

Fast Fact ⋆Read Aloud⋆

People have long believed that feelings come "from the heart," so the simple red heart shape became the symbol of Valentine's Day.

⋆Talk About ⋆It   Why would the heart be a place where your feelings come from? Do you think feelings come from other parts of the body such as the hands, the brain, or the mouth?

In Other Words ⋆Read Aloud⋆

Who is the little boy, Cupid, and why does he shoot arrows? According to Roman mythology, Cupid is the son of Venus, the goddess of love. Cupid shoots gods and humans with his arrows, causing them to fall in love. Cupid comes from the Latin word *cupido*, meaning "desire."

The Valentine's Day Caring Game `Social Studies`

During the week before Valentine's Day, ask students for suggestions about how they might do something helpful and caring for a classmate or the entire class. You might want to help them by giving age-appropriate and child-sensitive prompts. Write down and put these "caring tasks" in a box on your desk. Throughout Valentine's Day, ask students to pick out and complete one caring task. When a student completes a caring task, he or she receives a little token of thanks . . . because you care too!

⋆TIP⋆   Make a "caring tasks" box by decorating a tissue box with red construction paper, stickers, and other decorations. Better yet, let all students make one—it's a great keepsake for holding valentines!

Valentine's Day

Secret Valentine!, page 76 `Language Arts`

Reinforce the concept of caring—and make sure every student gets a valentine this year—with this fun game of "secret valentine." Distribute copies of the reproducible and have students write their names and favorite hobbies and colors at the top. Collect the papers and fold them in half to hide the name. Distribute, making sure no one gets his or her own name. With this information, each student can then specially decorate and cut out the card provided for the "secret valentine." Collect the finished cards and pass out the valentines. Students will love guessing whom they're from!

Reproducible

To:

Here's a card from me to you,
In your favorite color, too.

Have some fun,
and please be mine—
From your secret valentine.

★ Book Link

My Book of Funny Valentines by Margo Lundell (Cartwheel Books, 1993). Picture book, all ages. Valentine sentiments that children will understand.

Around the World *Read Aloud*

Did you ever have a secret valentine? If you lived in Denmark, your secret valentine would play this little game. He or she would write you a rhyme in a card but instead of signing the card, your secret valentine would leave dots—one dot for each of the letters of his or her name. If you guessed your secret valentine's identity, you would receive a special colored egg on Easter! But you wouldn't take this card, called a *goekkebrev*, too seriously; in Danish, the name means a "joking letter."

Funny Valentine Exchange `Language Arts`

"Roses are red, violets are blue, sugar is sweet and so are you!" Using this traditional four-line rhyme as a springboard, let each student write a funny valentine about friends, school, or family. FOR OLDER STUDENTS: Challenge students to create a series of rhyming Valentine's Day notes among imaginary characters in a class (see examples below).

Roses are red
Violets are blue
I signed all my cards
(Now what do I do?)
—Thomas

Some cards are red
Some cards are blue
I gave Paige a pink one
With hearts on it too
—Ashley

Red cards are great
Pink cards are fun
Ashley's my best friend
She gets the best one!
—Paige

Violets are blue
Roses are red
I think Thomas likes me
I think I like Ned....
—Maria

Petals are soft
But stalks are hard
I'll trade my heart candy
for Ned's Green Serpent card
—Jake

Fire breath is red
Dragons are blue
I wanted Ned's card
And Luke's candy too!
—Liam

Lilies are white
Shamrocks are green
The card says "be mine"
...So what does that mean?
—Ned

Clear skies are blue
Rain clouds are gray
My students are wonderful
Happy Valentine's Day!
—Mrs. Jackson

100th Day of School

Varies in February • United States

Hurray for the 100th day of school! Schools around the country celebrate this day, usually in mid-February. It offers a fun break from the usual routine and an opportunity to reinforce math skills with games based on the number 100.

> Having a successful 100th day might require starting the activities on day 98 or 99.

★ Book Links

100th Day Worries by Margery Cuyler (Simon & Schuster, 2000). Picture book, all ages. A little girl worries about bringing the right 100th day of school items to class.

One Hundred Hungry Ants by Elinor J. Pinczes (Scholastic, 1993). Picture book, easy. Learn simple division with the help of some cute little ants.

One Hundred Is a Family by Pam Muñoz Ryan (Hyperion, 1994). Picture book, all ages. A simple lesson in numbers adds up to a message about the importance of teamwork in a community.

★ Teacher Resources

Fresh & Fun 100th Day of School by Jacqueline Clarke (Scholastic, 2001). For grades K–2. Many cross-curriculum activities, book suggestions, and teacher tips for your day's event.

50 Thematic Songs Sung to Your Favorite Tunes by Meish Goldish (Scholastic, 1999). For grades K–2.

One Hundred-athon `Math`

Give teams of students 100 of someting—for instance, pretzels, raisins, paper clips, or buttons. Challenge them to complete a project using those objects and the number 100. For example:

★ 100 raisins forming the number 100

★ pretzel-stick frame around the number 100

★ a 100-paper clip chain

★ a 100-button necklace

FOR OLDER STUDENTS: Have each student work on an individual 100-piece construction project at home. Give students 100 minutes to complete the project. Let them share their project with the class, and have fellow students reward (with 100 claps of applause!) uniqueness and creativity.

Say Cheers to the 100 Days of School! `Language Arts` `Math`

Pour cups of root beer and sing to the tune of "Ninety-Nine Bottles of Beer on the Wall." FOR OLDER STUDENTS: Make up new verses with addition and subtraction problems that add up to 100!

~ 100 Days of School ~

100 days of school in all,
100 days of school,
We managed to count a large
     amount,
100 days of school in all!

How did we get to 100 days?
100 days of school?
We started the fun with number 1,
Counting the days of school in all!

1 day of school at first,
Then 2, then 3, then 4.
We got up to 10, but didn't stop
     then.

We went to 100 days in all!
20, 30, 40 days,
50 days and more!
60, 70, 80, 90,
Up to 100 days in all!

100 days of school in all,
100 days of school,
We managed to count a large
     amount,
100 days of school in all!

—from *50 Thematic Songs Sung to Your Favorite Tunes*

Presidents' Day

Third Monday in February • United States

This is the official national holiday to honor the achievements of former U.S. presidents—a great civics lesson for all.

Fast Fact *Read Aloud*

Presidents' Day originally began as two holidays in February to honor the birthdays of two great presidents: George Washington (February 22) and Abraham Lincoln (February 12). Elected in 1789, George Washington was our first president. Abraham Lincoln, our sixteenth president, was elected in 1860. They were both great leaders during very hard times. General George Washington led our country to defeat Great Britain during the American Revolution. Abraham Lincoln was elected when the northern and the southern states were at odds over many issues, especially slavery. The Civil War began, and with Abraham Lincoln's guidance, the northern states won. Lincoln signed the Emancipation Proclamation, which began the process to abolish legalized slavery.

Counting on Famous Presidents, page 77 `Math`

Abraham Lincoln and George Washington are important presidents—and familiar faces on U.S. currency. Teach about these coins and bills and enjoy some challenging math problems with this reproducible activity. (Answers are on page 126.) FOR YOUNGER STUDENTS: Include only the one-dollar bill and penny in math problems. FOR OLDER STUDENTS: Have students quiz each other with their own math problems ("What do five Lincoln bills, four Washington coins, three Lincoln coins, and two Washington bills add up to?").

Reproducible

Fast Fact *Read Aloud*

Do you want to be president of the United States? If you do, there are only three rules. Our forefathers wrote these rules in the Constitution right after the American Revolution to make sure that the president was dedicated to the United States. First, you have to be born in the United States or a commonwealth (such as Puerto Rico or the Virgin Islands). You can also be a "natural born" citizen—you can be born in another country if at least one of your parents is a U.S. citizen and has lived here. Second, you have to have lived in the United States for at least fourteen years. One more thing: You have to be at least thirty-five years old.

Talk About It Name someone you know who could run for president (remember that he or she must meet all the criteria or rules). How many more years do you have to wait before you can run for president?

For more information about elections, see Election Day in November on page 31.

★ Book Links

George Washington by Philip Abraham (Grolier, 2002). Picture book, easy. This simple account of his life is written for younger students.

Abraham Lincoln by Amy L. Cohn and Suzy Schmidt (Scholastic, 2002). Picture book, all ages. This enjoyable story is perfect for elementary school reading—the book is even tall!

★ Web Link

For a kid-friendly look at presidential elections, check out **www.kidsnewsroom.com**.

★ Teacher Resources

Famous Americans (Scholastic, 1997). Twenty-two reproducible read-aloud plays bring history to life. Includes plays about Washington and Lincoln.

The New Big Book of U.S. Presidents by Todd Davis and Marc Frey (Running Press, 2001). Includes biographies and a historical timeline of the presidency.

Presidents' Day

★ **Book Link**

If I Were President
by Catherine Stier (Albert Whitman, 1999). Picture book, all ages. A child dreams of being president and teaches readers about the job and its responsibilities.

★ **Web Link**

Visit **www.whitehousekids.gov**, the official White House Web site for kids. Learn all about the current president, first lady, and even the first pets. It contains teacher guides, and links to biographies of past presidents (suited for older students).

The Presidential Oath ~ of Office ~

I do solemnly swear I will faithfully execute the office of President of the United States, and will to the best of my ability, preserve, protect, and defend the Constitution of the United States.

Presidential Paper Plate `Social Studies`

Take this opportunity to learn about the job of the president of the United States. On the chalkboard or chart paper, record at least 25 facts about the job of the president. Let each student choose one fact to write on a plain white paper plate (younger students may need help). Using the space around the writing, students can draw a picture of the president doing this part of the job. Then have them decorate the rim with red and blue designs, star stickers, and other patriotic symbols. When the plates are dry, hang them up as a bulletin board display or serve the president's favorite snack foods (see Web Link) on them.

The president signs bills that Congress passes to make them laws.

Fast Fact ✷Read Aloud✷

Although the United States president is voted into office every four years on Election Day in November (see page 31), the new leader officially starts the first term about two months later on January 20. On this important day, called Inauguration Day, the president-elect places a hand on a bible, and makes a promise to the people to be a good and faithful president. This promise is the Oath of Office. The oath comes right from a section of the U.S. Constitution. The Chief Justice, the country's head judge, holds the bible.

✷Talk About ✷It   What are other oaths or important promises people might make?

In Other Words

The inauguration—which means the introduction or beginning—is the president's first day of work. The type of ceremony is the president's choice; some have held a big public ceremony on the steps of the Capitol building, while others have taken their oath in private quarters in the White House.

America Celebrates

Presidents' Day is a national holiday, but some states have different names for it—for instance, Minnesota calls it Founders Day. Some states don't recognize Lincoln's birthday at all, because of his stand against the southern states in the Civil War.

✷Talk About ✷It   How does your state celebrate Presidents' Day?

Mark Your Calendar

The week around February 22 is also known as Brotherhood Week. It was created to build awareness of different cultures, religions, and peoples. It is held around George Washington's birthday because he is a symbol of the birth of our nation.

Carnival

Several days in February or March (before Ash Wednesday, the first day of Lent) • Latin Americans worldwide/Christian

Enjoy a colorful cultural lesson about this popular Latin American celebration and provide some important background on the solemn days that lead up to Easter.

Fast Fact

Lent is the period of forty days (excluding Sundays) leading up Easter, when Jesus Christ, whom Christians believe was the son of God, is said to have risen from the dead. It is a serious time. During this period of sacrifice, many Christians give up something they care about, such as a special food or hobby. On Ash Wednesday, the first day of Lent, western Christian churches (especially Roman Catholic, Anglican, and Lutheran) traditionally hold services during which congregants receive ashes in the shape of a cross on their foreheads. The ashes stand for sin, the mistakes that people make.

To learn about the Lenten calendar, see page 8.

Traditions Today

Carnival is the annual Latin American celebration that occurs right before the beginning of Lent. Rio de Janeiro hosts the most magnificent Carnival festival of its kind. Several Brazilian schools spend the whole year creating Carnival costumes and floats and rehearsing a dance for the festival. Samba is the dance of Brazil. The dancers wear bright and beautiful costumes and dance to rhythms made with cymbals and drums. Brazilians fill the streets to watch the parade. Then everyone sits in the Sambodrome, a huge stadium, to watch the dance.

In Other Words

Carnival comes from the Latin words *carne vale*, which mean "good-bye meat." During the forty days of Lent, Christians were originally not allowed to eat meat. Carnival was the last chance to enjoy it. Today Christians may forgo meat only on Fridays during Lent.

A Classroom Carnival `Social Studies`

Put together a fast but festive Carnival celebration.

★ **Costumes:** Ask students to wear brightly-colored clothing. Boys can wear straw hats, and girls can wear flowers in their hair. (Make the Guadalupe roses on page 48. Try using tissue paper in different colors.)

★ **Music:** For maracas, decorate small paper bags with bright colors, fill the bags with dried beans, and tie them at the top with yarn. Shake them to the samba beat: 1–2–3 & 4 & 5 & 6 & 7 & 8 & …

★ **Dance!** Carnival dancing is free-form, so it's especially easy for students. Form a conga line by having students place their hands on the waist of the person in front of them. Have them walk to the beat of Latin-American dance music and swing their hips out with each step. Urge the leader to move the line around the room, weaving through the space.

Around the World

Here are some other pre-Lenten events around the world.

Great Britain: The British call this holiday Pancake Day. When the bells at the local church start ringing, apron-wearing women holding pancakes in frying pans run to the church while flipping their pancakes. The first to arrive to feed the bell ringer gets the special Kiss of Peace. British women have been running with their breakfast on this day for more than 500 years.

Carnival

★ **Book Link**

Gaston Goes to Mardi Gras by James Rice (Pelican, 2000). Picture book, all ages. A short overview of traditional Mardi Gras celebration in New Orleans.

Germany: During Fastnacht, translated as the Evening of the Fast, the ritual is to bake large rectangular doughnuts filled with molasses for dunking in tea.

United States: Originally a French Carnival celebration, Mardi Gras came to New Orleans, Louisiana, in 1699. Since then, Mardi Gras has taken on its own traditions. Today, it's an event filled with parades, dances, and feasts. People marching in parades wear elaborate costumes and special masks. These "maskers" throw trinkets such as plastic beads, cups, and coins to the crowd. The popular treat of the day is the King Cake—a cinnamon-topped round cake decorated with purple, green, and gold (yellow) icing. Baked inside the cake is a tiny plastic baby. New Orleans tradition says that the person whose piece holds the prize will host the next year's King Cake party. Though Mardi Gras is a one-day event in France, the American celebration in the Southeast lasts for about two weeks leading up to Lent.

In Other Words

Mardi Gras is French for "fat Tuesday." The "fat" refers to an ancient European spring festival tradition of parading a plump ox through the streets in hopes of fertile crops.

Leap Year Day

February 29 • Worldwide

Leap year occurs every four years when an extra day, February 29, is added to the calendar. Whether it's a leap year or not, reserve the last day of February to talk about the days and months of the year.

In Other Words

Why is a year with an extra day in February called a "leap year"? A long time ago, the English courts would not recognize the extra day in the year. They would "leap" over the day in their records.

Holiday History

Earth's revolution around the sun is the basis of our calendar. But since it takes 365.242199 days for Earth to circle the sun, the original "solar calendar" years came up short. The Roman calendar, developed in the seventh century B.C., divided the year into 10 months or 298 days. Later, two more months, January (29 days) and February (28 days), were added. Still short on days, an extra month was added every other year. The calendar still lost time. By 46 B.C., it was about one season behind. To set the calendar right, Julius Caesar gave that year 445 days, then established the new Julian calendar with 365 days plus an additional day every four years in February. But by 1582, the calendar was 10 days ahead! Pope Gregory XIII, realizing that there were too many "leap year days," then removed 10 days from that year. To correct the problem in the future, he created the Gregorian calendar that would have no leap year day in any year ending in 00 unless it was divisible by 400. We still use this system today.

> ### Thirty Days
> ### ~ Hath September ~
>
> Thirty days hath September,
> April, June, and November.
> All the rest have thirty-one
> Save February alone
> Which hath twenty-eight, in fine,
> Till leap-year gives it twenty-nine.
>
> —Richard Grafton (1570)

★Talk About ★It Is this year a leap year according to the Gregorian calendar? If not, when will the next leap year occur?

Name _____

December Holidays

Date _____

December Match-Up

Can you match each winter holiday symbol below to its name?
Draw a line to match the word to its picture.

candle
dreidel
gelt
kinara
menorah
noisemaker
piñata
mkeka
resolutions
rose
star
reindeer
tree

I will try to...

BONUS: Which symbol goes with which holiday? Write the name of the symbols next to the appropriate holiday shown below. Some symbols might belong with more than one holiday.

Hanukkah symbols: _____ _____ _____ _____

Our Lady of Guadalupe symbols: _____

Christmas symbols: _____ _____ _____

Kwanzaa symbols: _____ _____ _____

Las Posadas symbols: _____ _____

New Year's Eve symbols: _____ _____

(Answers: See page 126.)

The Scholastic Big Book of Holidays Around the Year   Scholastic Teaching Resources

Christmas

Advent Activity Jar

Count down the days to the holiday break with these and other fun activities. (For directions on making an Advent Activity Jar, see page 49.)

Learn how to say "Merry Christmas" in other languages, such as Spanish—Feliz Navidad, and French—Joyeuse Noël.	Name five words that rhyme with tree. Use them to write a holiday poem.
Decorate a holiday card for someone in your class.	Make a snowflake: Fold a square and cut out shapes along the fold and edges.
Take a survey of three friends or family members to learn what their favorite holiday songs are.	Draw a picture of a scene from your favorite holiday story.
Tell this joke to your class: Why is Christmas like a lion at the beach? Answer: Both have sandy claws! Tell another favorite holiday joke.	List five new uses for a candy cane.
Design a "Holiday Spirit" award. Give it to someone in class who shares, cares, and cooperates.	Describe your favorite holiday meal in a short paragraph or with a picture.
Make an ornament by tracing your hand on red poster board. Cut it out, decorate it, and punch a hole in the top. Tie a ribbon through the hole.	Fill some glasses with different amounts of water. Tap the glasses with a spoon to make music. Play your favorite holiday song!
Give a gift from your heart: Do something to help at school without being asked.	Say this three times fast: "Santa's sassy sheep." Create more holiday tongue twisters and challenge your classmates!

The Scholastic Big Book of Holidays Around the Year Scholastic Teaching Resources

Name _____

Date _____

New Year's Resolutions

Ask three family members or friends to make a resolution for the coming year. Write their names and resolutions below. Then write your own at the bottom of the page. Decorate the resolutions, cut them out, and post them where you, your family, and friends can see them!

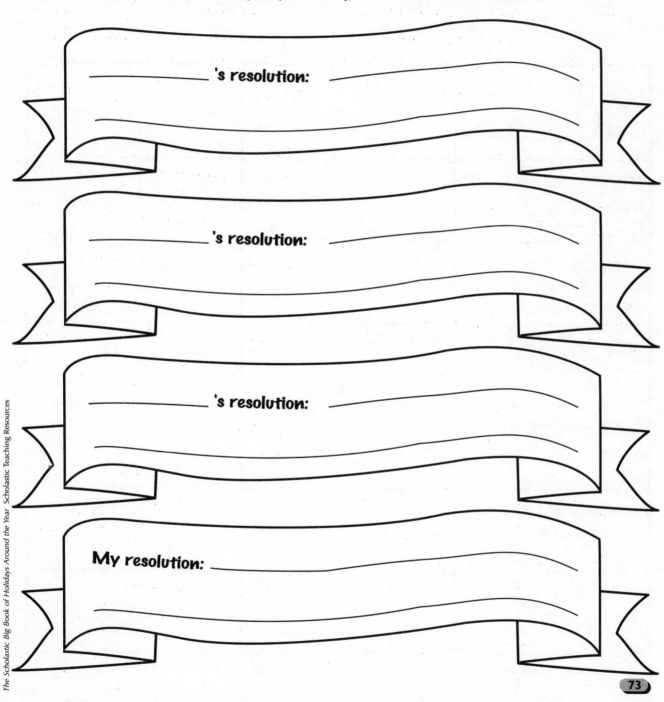

_____ 's resolution: _____

_____ 's resolution: _____

_____ 's resolution: _____

My resolution: _____

Martin Luther King Jr's Birthday

Name _____

Date _____

Alike and Different

Dr. King believed that people can be different but still work together for the same goals: peace and justice. Fill in the Alike and Different chart to show how you and a classmate are both similar and unique.

_____ _____
Our Names

	How we are alike	How we are different
Appearance: hair, skin, eyes, height, and so on		
Personality		
Family and heritage		
Things we like to do		
Favorite books or movies		
Favorite foods		

On the back of the page, draw a picture of one way the two of you are alike and one way you are different.

The Scholastic Big Book of Holidays Around the Year Scholastic Teaching Resources

African-American Hero Collector Cards

Many African Americans throughout history changed our world. Create collector cards to learn about them! Fill in the name of your hero and then draw a picture of him or her in the oval. Complete the rest of the card. Then cut it out and fold it so the writing is on the outside. Glue or tape the card together. Trade cards with your classmates!

African-American Hero

_____

Year of birth–Year of death
(Example: 1900–1972. If your hero is still alive, leave the last date blank.)

This card was created by _____

Name of hero: _____

Date of birth: _____

Place of birth: _____

Type of work: _____

Great accomplishments: _____

_____

The reason our lives are better today because of this hero: _____

_____

_____

Secret Valentine!

Make Valentine's Day a special day for a classmate. Here's how.

★ Find your secret valentine's name and favorite hobby and color in the top right corner of the card. ★ Fill in his or her name and decorate this card with a picture of your secret valentine doing his or her favorite hobby. Be sure to use your secret valentine's favorite color. ★ Cut out the card, fold it in half, and give it back to your teacher. ★ Next you will get a valentine like this from a classmate. Can you guess who sent it?

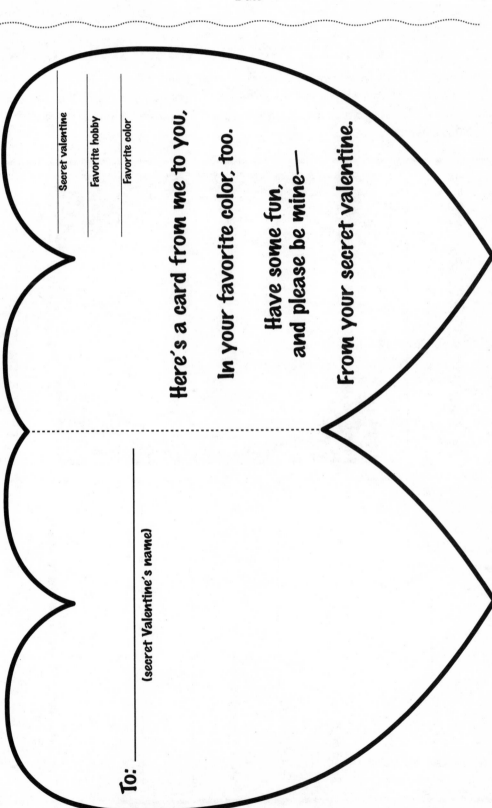

Secret valentine _____

Favorite hobby _____

Favorite color _____

Here's a card from me to you,

In your favorite color, too.

Have some fun,
and please be mine—

From your secret valentine.

To: _____
(secret Valentine's name)

The Scholastic Big Book of Holidays Around the Year Scholastic Teaching Resources

Name _____

Date _____

Counting on Famous Presidents

Can you solve these money riddles? Draw a line from the riddle to the correct bill or coin and write the answers on the lines.

A. I show a portrait of the first U.S. president. I am also called a "single" when people count me.

I am $ _____. The U.S. president is _____.

B. I am the smallest unit of money you would find in your pocket. The U.S. president on my face served his term during the Civil War.

I am $ _____. The U.S. president is _____.

C. Four of my units make $20. The president on my face delivered the famous Gettysburg Address on November 19, 1863.

I am $ _____. The U.S. president is _____.

D. I am one fourth of the smallest bill. The U.S. president I feature served as a general in the Revolutionary War.

I am $ _____. The U.S. president is _____.

Add up the presidents and see how much money you've got! First write the number sentence, then write the answer.

1. Two Lincoln bills plus two Washington bills

_____ + _____ + _____ + _____ = $_____

2. Two Washington bills plus four Washington coins

_____ + _____ + _____ + _____ + _____ + _____ = $_____

3. Three Lincoln bills plus six Lincoln coins

_____ + _____ + _____ + _____ + _____ + _____ + _____ + _____ + _____ = $_____

4. One Washington coin minus five Lincoln coins

_____ – (_____ + _____ + _____ + _____ + _____) = $_____

5. One Lincoln bill plus three Washington bills plus two Washington coins minus one Lincoln coin

_____ + _____ + _____ + _____ + _____ – _____ = $_____

Now make up your own presidential money problems and challenge your classmates!

(Answers: See page 126.)

The Scholastic Big Book of Holidays Around the Year   Scholastic Teaching Resources

Spring Calendar
March

March 1–31	MUSIC IN OUR SCHOOLS MONTH	United States	79
March 1–31	YOUTH ART MONTH	United States	79
March 1–31	WOMEN'S HISTORY MONTH	United States	80
Week around March 2	READ ACROSS AMERICA	United States	81
March 3	HINA MATSURI	Japan	82
March 17	ST. PATRICK'S DAY	Ireland and worldwide/Christian	83
March or April	PASSOVER	Jewish	84
A Sunday in March or April	EASTER	Christian	85

April

April 1–30	NATIONAL POETRY MONTH	United States	87
April 1	APRIL FOOL'S DAY	United States, England, Scotland, France, other countries	88
April 8	BUDDHA'S BIRTHDAY	Buddhist	89
April 14	PAN AMERICAN DAY	North America, Central America, South America	90
Fourth Thursday in April	TAKE OUR DAUGHTERS AND SONS TO WORK DAY	United States	90
Week around April 22	NATIONAL COIN WEEK	United States	91
Week around April 22	TV TURNOFF WEEK	United States	92
April 22 (some states vary)	EARTH DAY/ARBOR DAY	Worldwide	92

May

May 1–31	ASIAN-PACIFIC HERITAGE MONTH	United States	94
May 1–31	PHYSICAL FITNESS AND SPORTS MONTH	United States	96
Week of May 5	NATIONAL POSTCARD WEEK	United States	96
May 1 (and throughout spring)	MAY DAY AND SPRING FESTIVALS AROUND THE WORLD	United States and Europe, India, Israel, Pakistan, Thailand, Spain	97
May 5	CINCO DE MAYO	Mexico	99
Second Sunday in May	MOTHER'S DAY	United States, France, Sweden, other countries	100
Last Monday in May	MEMORIAL DAY	United States	101

 Spring Reproducibles

 For great ideas for celebrating students' birthdays, see Birthday Celebrations Around the World in June on pages 117–118.

Music in Our Schools Month

March 1–31 • United States

Music can soothe and inspire—and engage your auditory learners! Make it a goal to incorporate rhythm into your lessons this month and throughout the year.

Learning to Music Social Studies   Language Arts   Math

★ **Writing:** Each day for a week during journal writing time, play a different kind of music (e.g., classical, jazz, gospel, New Age). Have students share examples of how the music inspired their writing and compare their entries from one day to the next. How did they use words to respond to each type of music? Can they identify rhythm in their writing?

★ **U.S. Geography:** Sing "This Land Is Your Land" with the class. Have students locate the various regions, features, and places in the lyrics. Discuss Woody Guthrie's message to Americans. Invite a guitar-playing guest for a folk-song sing-along.

★ **Fractions:** Clap, drum, or slap your lap in slow beats in fours: 1-2-3-4; 1-2-3-4. Students can "drum" each beat of "Twinkle, Twinkle Little Star" to identify eighth notes in a bar of music.

★ Book Links

This Land Is Your Land by Woody Guthrie, illustrated by Kathy Jakobsen (Little, Brown, 1998). Picture book, easy. The famous song is brought to life with simple folk art.

The Sound That Jazz Makes by Carole Boston (Walker & Company, 2000). Picture book, easy. The history of jazz is introduced to children, with vibrant illustrations.

★ Teacher Resources

Kids Make Music! Clapping & Tapping from Bach to Rock! by Avery Hart and Paul Mantell (Williamson, 1993).

Teaching American History With Favorite Folk Songs by Tracey West (Scholastic, 2001). Twelve Songs on CD, song sheets, and activities that teach about U.S. history.

Youth Art Month

March 1–31 • United States

Students benefit from looking at the world through an artist's eyes—and exploring artists' unique ways of expressing themselves.

Making Colors   Art

How do you make your favorite color? Let students enjoy learning how to mix colors. Give them paintbrushes and acrylic paints in the three primary colors: yellow, blue, and red. Have them mix and match to create orange (red and yellow), green (yellow and blue), purple (red and blue), and brown (yellow, blue, and red). Be sure to provide each student with his or her own palette (a styrofoam tray), a canister of water for rinsing the brushes, and a sponge to soak up excess water on the brushes. As they mix colors, remind students to keep the primary colors separate and to thoroughly rinse the brush between mixing. Don't want to break out the paints? Try overlapping color transparencies on an overhead projector. FOR OLDER STUDENTS: Add black and white paints, and show students how to darken and lighten colors.

★ Book Links

I Am an Artist by Pat Lowery Collins (Millbrook Press, 1994). Picture book, all ages. A child shows how to see the world from an artist's perspective.

The Art Box by Gail Gibbons (Holiday House, 1998). Picture book, easy. The tools of an artist are illustrated with simple and colorful text.

★ Teacher Resource

In the Paint by Patrick Ewing and Linda L. Louis (Abbeville Press, 1999). All grades. Ways to engage students in age-appropriate, creative work and easily manage painting in the classroom. Includes tips from a basket-ball pro and an art educator.

Women's History Month

March 1–31 • United States

Reinforce social studies and multicultural lessons by learning about the accomplishments of women throughout history.

★ Book Links

Scholastic Encyclopedia of Women in the United States by Sheila Keenan (Scholastic, 2002). Reference book, intermediate. Biographies of more than 250 women throughout American history.

You Want Women to Vote, Lizzie Stanton? by Jean Fritz (Penguin Putnam, 1995). Chapter book, intermediate. Part of the Unforgettable Americans series, this book makes Stanton's plight for women's rights accessible and enjoyable.

★ Web Link

The National Women's History Project's Web site at **www.nwhp.org** includes an annual theme, biographies of legendary women, a historical timeline, the "learning place" for educational materials, and more.

Holiday History ★Read Aloud★

Did you know that at one time women couldn't go to college, vote in elections, hold government office, or even own property in the United States? It took the hard work of women such as Elizabeth Cady Stanton and the leaders of the Women's Suffrage movement to give women the rights they have today.

> ### ~ EXCERPT ~
> Men, their rights, and nothing more;
> Women, their rights, and nothing less.
> —Women's Rights movement battle cry

★Reproducible★

Famous Women in History Mobiles, page 103 `Language Arts`

Show classroom pride in women's history by creating and displaying simple mobiles of historic facts hung on wire clothing hangers. Have students research facts about selected women in history. Cutout fact boxes and directions for making the mobiles are on the reproducible page. Hang the mobiles around the classroom throughout the month. FOR YOUNGER STUDENTS: Read aloud short biographies and create large shapes for students to illustrate. FOR OLDER STUDENTS: Have students write a résumé for the figure they are researching to hang near the mobile. The résumé should include important achievements, skills, and education credentials.

Here is a brief list of some famous women whom students can select for their mobiles or for a class timeline.

- ★ Joan of Arc, religious martyr (1412–1451)
- ★ Elizabeth I, Queen of England (1533–1603)
- ★ Jane Austen, author (1775–1817)
- ★ Sacagawea, Native American guide (1789–1812?)
- ★ Harriet Tubman, conductor on Underground Railroad (1821–1913)
- ★ Elizabeth Cady Stanton, women's rights activist (1815–1902)
- ★ Susan B. Anthony, women's rights activist (1820–1906)
- ★ Florence Nightingale, nurse (1820–1910)
- ★ Clara Barton, battlefield nurse (1821–1912)
- ★ Marie Curie, physicist (1867–1934)
- ★ Maria Montessori, educator (1870–1952)

- ★ Helen Keller, teacher and advocate for the blind (1880–1968)
- ★ Eleanor Roosevelt, first lady (1884–1962)
- ★ Martha Graham, dancer (1894–1991)
- ★ Georgia O'Keeffe, painter (1887–1986)
- ★ Amelia Earhart, pilot (1897–1937)
- ★ Golda Meir, Israeli prime minister (1898–1978)
- ★ Margaret Bourke-White, photographer (1904–1971)
- ★ Mother Teresa, Catholic nun (1910–1997)
- ★ Mildred "Babe" Didrikson Zaharias, track and field/golf star (1911–1956)
- ★ Eva Perón, Argentine first lady (1919–1952)
- ★ Margaret Thatcher, British prime minister (1925–)
- ★ Jacqueline Kennedy Onassis, first lady (1929–1994)

Read Across America

Week around March 2 • United States

This is the official week in the school year devoted to reading. Enjoy the celebration—and its obvious benefits—all year long.

Mark Your Calendar

The week of March 3 is also Children's Authors and Illustrators Week! Celebrate their talents in your classroom every week. See also National Children's Book Week in November on page 35.

Read Across America Map `Social Studies` `Language Arts`

Encourage students to literally "read across America" by choosing stories about different places in the country. After reading a book, ask each student to write his or her name on a precut star, which can be die-cut from multicolored construction paper and taped or tacked onto the map. On a wall map, help students find and attach their stars next to the place where their books were set. Your "stars" will take pride as the map fills up with their reading accomplishments.

Reproducible

Books From Across America, page 104 `Social Studies` `Language Arts`

How are other towns in our country different from where you live? Urge students to answer questions that explore the place where a book they've read is set with this reproducible companion to the Read Across America Map activity above. FOR YOUNGER STUDENTS: Read a story and answer the questions together. FOR OLDER STUDENTS: Using the information on the reproducible, ask students to create a brochure inviting tourists to visit the town. Have them decorate the brochure with their own illustrations of the main characters and scenes from the book.

★ Teacher Resources

Read Across America by Gloria Rothstein (Scholastic, 1997) and ***35 Best Books for Teaching U.S. Regions*** by Toni Buzzeo and Jan Kurtz (Scholastic, 2002). For grades 1–4 and 4–8. Information-packed teaching guides for exploring seven U.S. regions through popular children's literature and young adult literature.

★ Web Link

Read Across America is a project of the National Education Association. The organization's Web site, **www.nea.org**, includes useful activities for teachers.

Here are some great books to get students started on their reading journeys across America. For each region, a picture book and a chapter book are listed.

New England
- ★ *Miss Rumphius* by Barbara Cooney (Viking, 1986). Picture book.
- ★ *Lyddie* by Katherine Paterson (Puffin, 1991). Chapter book.

Middle Atlantic
- ★ *Tar Beach* by Faith Ringgold (Scholastic, 1991). Picture book.
- ★ *Homecoming* by Cynthia Voigt (Ballantine, 1996). Chapter book.

Southeast
- ★ *Bigmamas* by Donald Crews (Greenwillow, 1991). Picture book.
- ★ *Roll of Thunder, Hear My Cry* by Mildred D. Taylor (Puffin, 1976). Chapter book.

Southwest
- ★ *Roxaboxen* by Alice McLerran (Scholastic, 1991). Picture book.
- ★ *Out of the Dust* by Karen Hesse (Scholastic, 1998). Chapter book.

Midwest
- ★ *Thunder Cake* by Patricia Polacco (Scholastic, 1990). Picture book.
- ★ *The Watsons Go to Birmingham—1963* by Christopher Paul Curtis (Yearling, 1995). Chapter book.

Mountain
- ★ *The Legend of the Indian Paintbrush* by Tomie dePaola (Scholastic, 1988). Picture book.
- ★ *Dragon's Gate* by Lawrence Yep (HarperTrophy, 1993). Chapter book.

Pacific
- ★ *Grandfather's Journey* by Allen Say (Houghton Mifflin, 1993). Picture book.
- ★ *The Ballad of Lucy Whipple* by Karen Cushman (HarperCollins, 1996). Chapter book.

Read Across America

Dr. Seuss Reading Corner `Language Arts`

Read Across America pays special homage to Theodore Seuss Geisel, a.k.a. Dr. Seuss, who was born on March 2, 1904. Invite family members, local leaders (the mayor, a police officer, even a store owner), older students, and others to read Dr. Seuss books with your class. Here are a few favorites and their themes.

★ ***And to Think That I Saw It on Mulberry Street*** (1937)
Imagination: "for I had a story that NO ONE could beat! And to think that I saw it on Mulberry Street! . . . "

★ ***Green Eggs & Ham*** (1960)
Trying new things: "I do so like green eggs and ham! Thank you! Thank you, Sam-I-am!"

★ ***The Lorax*** (1971)
Environmental protection: "Grow a forest. Protect it from axes that hack. Then the Lorax and all of his friends may come back."

Wearable Book Charts `Art` `Language Arts`

Chart reading progress with Cat in the Hat hats. Tape red construction paper to fit around the crown of each student's head. For the rim, use a large paper plate; trace the opening of the hat in the middle of the plate, cut out the circle, and tape it to fit around the top of the hat. With every book the student reads, add a white paper stripe around the top. Students can write the book title, author, and a short summary on the stripe.

Hina Matsuri

March 3 • Japan

This Japanese doll festival provides a valuable lesson in culture and collecting.

Fast Fact ★Read Aloud★

Hina Matsuri is the annual Girls' Festival—a special day in Japan devoted to girls and their dolls. On this day, Japanese girls receive beautiful hina dolls. But this is not a day for play! The dolls are displayed formally in a special room in the house for the family and visitors to admire. These dolls are

Boys shouldn't feel left out! Boys' Festival is celebrated May 5. See page 95.

added to the family set, which is often passed down from many generations. A traditional set is made to look like the emperor and his family and includes furniture and seasonal trees such as cherry blossoms and mandarins. Younger girls look forward to the day when they are old enough to set up the doll displays by themselves.

★Talk About ★It Do you have a doll or keepsake that's special? Did you get it at a special place or from a special person? Was it something handed down by a family member? Where do you keep or display it?

Traditions Today ★Read Aloud★

Some Japanese people believe that sickness or bad luck can be transferred and taken away through a doll. Families today practice this belief by taking the doll of a child who is sick to a special shrine. A priest says a prayer over the doll and puts it in a wooden boat with the dolls of other sick children. The dolls are then cast out to sea.

St. Patrick's Day

March 17 • Ireland and worldwide/Christian

This day celebrates St. Patrick, who converted many Irish to Christianity. He died on this date in the fifth century. It's now a holiday to enjoy kid-favorite traditions and celebrate pride in everyone's heritage.

Holiday History
Born in England in the fifth century, the man who would become Saint Patrick was taken to Ireland where he was sold as a slave and worked as a shepherd. Patrick's strong faith led him to become a missionary and introduce Christianity to the Irish. He is the patron saint of Ireland.

Traditions Today
On St. Patrick's Day, people celebrating call out, "Erin go bragh!" which is Gaelic for "Ireland forever." Gaelic is the language that was spoken in Ireland long ago. Today, most Irish people speak English.

Fast Fact
The shamrock, or three-leaf clover, is a symbol of St. Patrick's Day. Patrick used the leaves of the shamrock to help followers understand what Christians describe as the three parts of God: the Father, Son, and Holy Spirit.

Holiday History *Read Aloud*
According to legend, leprechauns are tiny elves who try to keep humans away from their pots of gold. In one story, an Irishman caught a leprechaun and made the elf show him the tree under which gold was buried. The Irishman tied a red handkerchief around the trunk of the tree so he would remember where the gold was buried, and then he went away to find a shovel. When he returned, the tricky leprechaun had tied a red handkerchief around every tree in the forest!

In Other Words
Leprechaun is a combination of the Gaelic words for "shoemaker" and "small person."

Proud to Be Irish—and Every Nationality!  Social Studies   Art
Whether you're Irish or not, St. Patrick's Day is a day to celebrate cultural heritage. Encourage students to ask their families for the name of one country where their ancestors lived. Have them point to these countries on a map. They can trace a line with their fingers from these countries to their hometowns to show how far their ancestors traveled! To celebrate their cultural heritage, let students make colorful flags on large adhesive-back stickers and wear the flags with pride all day long. FOR OLDER STUDENTS: Students can research the meaning of the colors and symbols of their flags.

★ **Book Link**
Patrick: Patron Saint of Ireland by Tomie dePaola (Holiday House, 1992). Picture book, all ages. The story of St. Patrick is revealed in priceless dePaola style.

★ **Web Link**
Find all the flags of the world on the World Flag Database at **www.flags.net**.

~ Irish Blessing ~
May your blessings outnumber the shamrocks that grow And may trouble avoid you wherever you go!

Passover

March or April (15th–21st day of Nisan) • Jews worldwide

This holiday celebrates the Exodus, a miraculous time when Jews fled Egypt and were finally free from slavery. It teaches a valuable lesson about the importance of belief and tradition.

For more about Judaism and the Jewish calendar, see page 7.

★ Book Links

The Passover Journey by Barbara Diamond Goldin (Viking Penguin, 1997). Picture book, intermediate. This book tells the story of Moses and the seder ritual.

The Matzah That Papa Brought Home by Fran Manushkin (Scholastic, 1995). Picture book, all ages. A modern family celebrates the Passover seder.

Holiday History ✳Read Aloud✳

The story of the flight of the Israelites from Egypt, read at the beginning of the first meal of Passover, begins with Moses. As an infant, Moses was put in a basket and set adrift at sea. Moses's Jewish parents did this to protect him from the evil pharaoh, the king of Egypt, who hated and enslaved Jews. The pharaoh's daughter found Moses at the sea's edge and raised him as her son. When Moses grew up, he led the Jews away from the pharaoh's army to freedom.

Traditions Today

The festival of Passover lasts for eight days. It begins with a meal called a seder. Special foods eaten during the meal symbolize the Jews' struggle for freedom and help tell the Passover story.

 Matzoh
(for the bread that did not rise during the escape)

 Parsley
(for dipping in the salt water, to symbolize the miraculous parting of the waters of the Red Sea so that the Jews could flee from Egypt)

Salt Water
(for the tears shed during slavery in Egypt)

 Egg
(for mourning, and for the coming of spring)

Wine
(for the joy of the Jews' release from slavery)

 Bitter Herbs
(for the bitterness of slavery)

 Charoset
(for the mortar of the Egyptian buildings the Jewish slaves were forced to build)

 Lamb Bone
(for lamb's blood, left on Jews' houses the night before they fled Egypt)

In Other Words

Matzoh (or matzah) is the Hebrew word for unleavened bread—bread made with dough that has not risen. Jewish people eat it to remind them of when the Jews fled Egypt and did not have time to let their bread rise.

Easter

A Sunday in March or April • Christians worldwide

A celebration of rebirth and renewal, Christians believe that Jesus was resurrected after his crucifixion. Although this theme may be challenging for young students, everyone can enjoy Easter's message of new life and the joy of springtime.

In Other Words
The word Easter may come from Osters, the name of the Roman goddess who was worshipped during spring festivals.

Mark Your Calendar
You might want to note some of the important days of Holy Week. Start with Palm Sunday, which is one week before Easter. For information about Ash Wednesday and the forty-day period before Easter, called Lent, see Carnival in February on pages 69–70.

★ **Palm Sunday:** The Bible says that on this day people cut down branches while awaiting Jesus's arrival in Jerusalem. Churches traditionally give out palm branches during their services.

★ **Maundy Thursday:** This is the day of the Last Supper, Jesus's last meal with his disciples.

★ **Good Friday:** This is the crucifixion day on which Jesus died.

★ **Easter Sunday:** Easter is the end of Lent. During the forty days of Lent, many people don't eat certain foods. The Easter meal is important because people "break lent" and can eat those foods again.

> Easter is the only Western holiday set by the phases of the moon. For more about the date of Easter according to the Gregorian calendar, see page 8.

★ Book Links

Peter Cottontail by Amanda Stephens (Cartwheel, 1994). Picture book, easy. This is the traditional story behind the Easter egg hunt.

The Easter Bunny That Overslept by Priscilla Friedrich (HarperCollins, 2002). Picture book, all ages. This engaging book retells the 1957 tale.

In Other Words
The word *maundy* is taken from the Latin *mandatum*, meaning "commandment." During the Last Supper, Jesus gave his followers a new commandment: to "love one another, even as I have loved you. . . ."

Holiday History
The Easter Parade has been a tradition since ancient times, but it was originally a dance to celebrate the coming of spring. People would put on new clothes, wear flowers, and then come together to dance outdoors for the new season.

Fast Fact *Read Aloud*
Many women and girls wear bonnets, which are fancy hats, to church on Easter Sunday. According to legend, the young girl who wears a new hat on Easter will have good luck and find love the next year.

America Celebrates
Children of all religions enjoy traditional egg hunts—a town event where colorful plastic eggs filled with treats are scattered in a park or field for all to collect and enjoy. The most famous American egg hunt is the White House Easter Egg Roll, held every Easter Monday on the South Lawn. Presidents have hosted this egg hunt for more than 120 years!

Easter

★ Book Links

The Egg Tree by Katherine Milhouse (Simon & Schuster, 1992). Picture book, all ages. This Caldecott-winning story tells about a Pennsylvania Dutch family and their Easter egg tree.

Chicken Sunday by Patricia Polacco (Penguin Putnam, 1995). Picture book, all ages. Though its theme is not Easter, this heartwarming story about friendship and tradition features an age-old Ukrainian tradition of egg decorating.

Celebrate Spring   `Social Studies`   `Science`   `Art`

Bring in the Easter Season with these simple activities.

★ **Signs of Spring Hats:** Help students glue paper constructions of flowers, plants, and other spring symbols onto an old hat or paper plate with ribbon attached (to tie under the chin).

★ **Observe and Illustrate:** Take paper and pencils or crayons outside and have students draw pictures of the new spring growth—leaves, flowers, and grasses. Help them find the names of each.

★ **Plant a Seed or Bulb:** Plant early-blooming flowers on your school grounds and let students observe and chart their growth (remember to ask permission first).

★ **Hold a Spring Festival Party:** For ideas, see May section on pages 97–98.

Around the World

Here are some Easter traditions from around the world.

Bulgaria: At Easter lunch, each person holds an egg and taps it against others' eggs. Whoever ends up with the last unbroken egg is believed to have a year of good luck.

Ethiopia: During the long church service of *Fassika*, priests chant prayers in an ancient language called Ge'ez while a drum beats.

Germany, France, Netherlands, Switzerland: Christian homes have "Easter trees"—bare branches stuck into potted dirt. Ribbons and hollowed-out eggs are hung from the branches.

Greece: Eggs are dyed red, which is believed to be a magical color. When the red shell is broken, a blessing is released. Greeks carry eggs around with them on Easter.

Mexico: During the weeks before Lent, children smash eggs over each other's heads! Luckily, these are cascarones, hollowed-out eggs filled with confetti.

Norway: Norwegians like to read all types of thrillers—*påskekrimmen*—during Easter break because of the violent and mysterious things that happened to Jesus.

Poland: According to Polish custom, on *Dyngus*, the Monday after Easter, children hide with buckets of water and douse unsuspecting passersby.

Ukraine: *Pysanky*, the Ukrainian Easter egg, dates back thousands of years. Symbolic designs on the egg include dots (for the stars in the heavens), spirals (the mystery of life and death), and unending lines (for the continuous thread of life). Simple designs can be made by using a fine-tipped tool to apply thin lines of melted candle wax to the shell before the egg is dyed.

United States: On Easter morning, the Easter Bunny visits the homes of Christian children, leaving baskets filled with candies and other treats. Traditionally, children decorate hard-boiled eggs by dipping them in colorful dye. Eggs or treats may be hidden around the house for children to find and collect. (Many Easter customs and traditions in the United States came from Germany—from coloring eggs to traditional egg hunts to the woven baskets filled with artificial grass.)

National Poetry Month

April 1–30 • United States

This month is the official celebration of poetry. Take this opportunity to dedicate time to reading poetry every day.

Holiday History
Created by the Academy of American Poets in 1996, National Poetry Month is a celebration of poetry and its place in our culture.

Number One, ~ Touch Your Tongue ~

Number one, touch your tongue.
Number two, touch your shoe.
Number three, touch your knee.
Number four, touch the floor.
Number five, learn to jive.
Number six, pick up sticks.
Number seven, go to heaven.
Number eight, shut the gate.
Number nine, touch your spine.
Number ten, do it all again!

—traditional street rhyme

Poetry in Motion   Language Arts
Students' first schoolyard exposure to poetry is often the street rhyme. Chanted while jumping rope, bouncing a ball, or just between giggles, street rhymes are great examples of simple rhythms and repeated sounds. Students can say the traditional rhyme at left while bouncing tennis balls; the trick is to "act out" the words using the hand that's bouncing the ball. FOR YOUNGER STUDENTS: Write down students' favorite street rhymes. Have them identify the rhyming word in each verse. Make up new verses together. FOR OLDER STUDENTS: Ask students to make up a similar game with the times table: "Two times two is four, now open up the door" and so on.

A Haiku Tea   Social Studies   Language Arts
Haiku is a Japanese form of poetry that is more than 500 years old. The traditional form is a short verse using seventeen syllables arranged in three lines: five on the first line, seven on the second, five on the third. Urge students to write haiku. Frame the poems on oversized construction paper that students have decorated. Invite family members to hear the haiku read aloud. Parent volunteers can bring in refreshments from Japanese cuisine such as rice crackers and (iced) tea. For a quick craft, make an origami teacup; see the Asian-Pacific Heritage Month reproducible on page 108.

In Other Words
Haiku is a Japanese word that loosely translates as "playful verse." To make the poem a true haiku, it must include a *kigo*—a word that reminds the reader of one of the four seasons.

Mark Your Calendar
Young People's Poetry Week, sponsored by the Children's Book Council, is the week of April 15. Encourage students to contribute poems to a class anthology or enter a poetry contest.

★ Book Links

Hey You! C'mere: A Poetry Slam by Elizabeth Swados (Arthur A. Levine Books, 2002). Picture book, all ages. This rap-like poetry book has a competitive twist.

Lunch Money and Other Poems About School by Carol Diggory Shields (Puffin, 1995). Picture book, all ages. Who can resist silly poems about school?

Miss Mary Mack and Other Children's Street Rhymes by Joanna Cole and Stephanie Calmenson (William Morrow, 1990). Picture book, all ages. This timeless collection is full of hand-clapping, jump-roping, ball-bouncing, and silly-time rhymes.

Don't Step on the Sky: A Handful of Haiku by Miriam Chaikin, illustrated by Hiroe Nakata (Henry Holt, 2002). Picture book, all ages. Simple and sweet modern haiku are accompanied by watercolor illustrations.

★ Teacher Resources
The National Poetry Month Web site at **www.poets.org/npm** includes the year's theme, teaching tips and ideas, and a database of poetry.

Instructor Magazine holds an annual poetry contest for grades K–8. Check out the entry information and this year's winners at **www.scholastic.com/instructor**.

April Fool's Day

April 1 • United States, England, Scotland, France, other countries

April Fool's Day, also known as All Fools' Day, is the one day of the year when playing innocent pranks and jokes on people is okay—and even educational!

★ Book Links

101 School Jokes by Lisa Eisenberg (Scholastic, 1987). Picture book, easy. Plenty of fun jokes about every aspect of school.

Mud Flat April Fools by James Stevenson (Greenwillow, 1988). Chapter book, all ages. Ten hilarious stories of April foolery make great read-alouds that will have kids in stitches.

Fast Fact

The tradition of April Fool's Day is said to come from France in the 1500s. According to the Julian calendar then, April 1 was New Year's Day. When the new Gregorian calendar was created in 1582, January 1 became New Year's Day. Since communication was slow, many people didn't hear about the change for a while so they continued to celebrate and exchange gifts on April 1. They were soon called "April fools," which led to the custom of playing tricks on this day.

In Other Words

There are many names for a fool around the world. In England, the person tricked is a *noddie* or *gawby*. In Scotland, that person is a *gowk* or a *cuckoo*. In France, the tricked person is a *poisson d'avril*, or "April fish"— the trick is to pin a paper fish on another person's back without getting caught.

April Fool's News   `Language Arts`

Stop the presses! This is the day when local newspapers may do some light-hearted spoofing of the news. Let students enjoy this tradition by looking for cartoons, articles on odd topics, or funny headlines in the paper and sharing them with the class. Then invite students to write an April Fool's school newsletter that pokes good-spirited fun at news from your school and around the world. Set up teams of students to write short articles. Make sure they are funny, but in good taste. Topics might include:

★ a review of a new (made-up) movie or book

★ what's on the lunch menu (cheese frogs and chocolate worms?)

★ current events (with a twist)

★ a new store in your town (free toys!)

★ an interview with a student or teacher (with some strange facts inserted—make sure to get permission from the interviewee)

FOR YOUNGER STUDENTS: Guide younger students as you write a funny class newsletter together.

Buddha's Birthday

April 8 • Buddhists worldwide

Introduce students to Buddhism, which encourages people to respect all living things and seeks a peaceful state called nirvana.

Holiday History *Read Aloud*

Siddhartha Gautama, known as the Buddha, lived more than 2,500 years ago in northern India. Although Siddhartha was a prince, he recognized the suffering of others and set out to help. He reached enlightenment, a state of understanding, and shared his teachings with many people. Buddhism follows his teachings. The Dalai Lama is the most famous teacher of Buddhism today.

★ Book Links

Hitz Demi captures the beauty and spirituality of India and Buddhism with quiet words and delicate paintings in these books:

Buddha Stories (Henry Holt, 1997). Picture book, all ages. Eleven *jakatas*, or fables, that the Buddha is said to have used in his teachings.

The Dalai Lama: A Biography of a Tibetan Spiritual Leader (Henry Holt, 1998). Picture book, intermediate. The story of the young boy who became the Dalai Lama.

Fast Fact

In the Buddha's first sermon to his followers, he spoke of eight steps that showed how they should live. An eight-spoked wheel naming these steps is the symbol of Buddhism.

Fast Fact *Read Aloud*

Buddhists do not pray because they do not believe in a god. Instead of prayer, Buddhists meditate, which is a state of deep concentration. This brings them enlightenment, an understanding of the world and one's place in it. Meditation takes years of practice. To stay focused, some people stare at small objects, and others quietly say the same words over and over.

Traditions Today

Here are some ways Buddhists from countries around the world celebrate the Buddha's birth, enlightenment, and death.

★ **Korea:** Koreans hold processions of paper lotus lanterns.

★ **Singapore:** People call this day Vesak Day and free caged animals.

★ **India:** Buddha Purnima includes homage to statues of Buddha, where visitors leave flowers, candles, and fruit.

Pan American Day

April 14 • North America, Central America, South America

This holiday, sanctioned by President Hoover in 1931, celebrates peace and respect among the countries in the Americas. It paves the way for a discussion of the importance of good relationships.

Fast Fact *Read Aloud*

It's important for us to get along with our neighbors. Just as you might borrow a toy or some food from a neighbor or visit a close family friend who is sick, it's also important for the United States to get along with Canada and the countries of Central America and South America. We trade goods with each other. We visit each other's countries. We need to stand together during times of war and peace. Pan American Day celebrates this unity.

Pan American Bingo `Social Studies`

Teach the names of the Pan American countries with a simple game of bingo. Write the names of fifteen countries in North America, South America, and Central America on the board and point them out on a map. Let students select nine countries to fill their bingo cards (one country name in each square) in any pattern they choose. While they are doing this, write the name of each country on a small piece of paper, fold it, and put it in a container. When everyone is ready, draw one country at a time and call out its name. The first student to fill the whole card is the winner. Have students swap cards and play again. FOR OLDER STUDENTS: Instead of calling out the country's name, point to its location on a blank world outline map and let students identify the matching name on their boards.

★TIP★ Make the bingo board by drawing nine boxes—three rows of three—on a sheet of 8½- by 11-inch paper. Photocopy and distribute it. Use any simple marker, such as pieces of scrap paper or beans.

Take Our Daughters and Sons To Work Day

Fourth Thursday in April • United States

The Ms. Foundation created Take Our Daughters to Work Day more than 30 years ago to give girls some much-needed exposure to the workplace. In 2003, the program was expanded to include boys. In or out of class, this is a day to encourage students to start dreaming big about their future careers.

My Day at Work, page 105 `Language Arts` *Reproducible*

Write a note to families to encourage them to take part in Take Our Daughters and Sons to Work Day. Ask participants to keep a journal of what they did all day and what they learned from the experience. The reproducible includes some starter questions. FOR YOUNGER STUDENTS: Ask students to tell about their day; you can use the answers (filled in by the parent) as prompts. FOR OLDER STUDENTS: Encourage students to make a journal book of the day; they can add photos or illustrations to show the day's events and the projects they accomplished.

Take Your Students to Work Day `Social Studies`

Dedicate the day to teaching students about your job and the jobs of others who work at your school. Ask the school principal, secretary, nurse, librarian, or any other staff member if one or two students can interview them or if they would visit the classroom for a whole-class interview. Have students complete a report about what they learned using the reproducible on page 105.

National Coin Week

Week of April 22 • United States

A study of our nation's currency is rich in history and offers plenty of real-life opportunities to reinforce math skills.

Fast Fact

The golden dollar is a new coin, put into circulation in the year 2000. It features the face of Sacagawea and her infant son Jean Baptiste. Sacagawea, a Shoshone Indian, served as a guide to the explorers Lewis and Clark.

★Talk About ★It What other famous faces in U.S. history appear on U.S. coins? (Penny: Abraham Lincoln; nickel: Thomas Jefferson; dime: Franklin Roosevelt; quarter: George Washington; half dollar: John F. Kennedy; silver dollar: Susan B. Anthony)

Coin Riddles `Math`

Coin riddles are a great way to learn about coins and reinforce math skills. Here are some examples.

★ I am two of the same coin. I equal 20 cents. (2 dimes)

★ I am two coins without presidents. I equal $2.00. (2 golden or silver dollars)

★ I am three coins. I am worth less than 10 cents. I have two different presidents. (1 nickel, 2 pennies)

★ I am seven coins. I am worth $1.93. I have at least one of each coin. (1 dollar, 1 half-dollar, 1 quarter, 1 dime, 1 nickel, 3 pennies)

Urge students to make up their own coin riddles to challenge their classmates.

★ Web Link

The United States Mint Web site at **www.usmint.gov** is a complete resource on the topic, including lesson plans and a quick review of how coins are made.

★ Teacher Resource

Teaching With State Quarters by Karen Baicker (Scholastic, 2003). Grades 2–5. Fifty nifty activities using these fun-to-collect coins to teach history, geography, math, and more.

Fast Fact *Read Aloud*

The 50 State Quarters Program introduces a new state quarter every ten weeks until 2008. The quarters are being introduced in the order in which the states joined the Union—so if you live in Alaska or Hawaii, you'll have to wait a while for your state coin. The state quarter has the same value as any other quarter (25 cents), but the design on the back features an important aspect of state history.

State Quarter Fact Sheet, page 106 `Language Arts` `Math` *Reproducible*

Ask students to bring in any state quarter and conduct some simple research on that state. (You might want to photocopy a state quarter for those who don't bring in their own.) Distribute copies of the reproducible page and use it to start a discussion. FOR YOUNGER STUDENTS: As a class, choose one state quarter—your own state or a nearby one with its own state quarter. Research and answer the questions together. FOR OLDER STUDENTS: Pass out large circles cut from white poster board; cover with foil and secure the foil with glue. Students can use permanent markers to draw the back of their state quarter on one side and then tape or glue to the other side a list of facts they've learned about their state. Hang the oversize quarters around your room during the week.

★Bulletin Board ★Idea Let students locate the states featured on their quarters on a wall map of the United States. They can place a small circle sticker with their initials on the featured states.

TV Turnoff Week

Week of April 22 • United States

Challenge students to turn off the tube at home and turn on more physically and mentally stimulating activities. Support their efforts with some fun and educational projects of your own.

★ Web Link

Download TV Turnoff Week posters for your school and community at **www.adbusters. org.** The site also offers TV-free activities and an "info arsenal" about harmful TV.

~ EXCERPT ~

It takes very little mental effort to follow a TV show. Kids raised on TV. . . are used to being spoon-fed information by television.
—from "Your child's brain wasn't built for all that TV" at **www.limiTV.org**

My Week Without TV, page 107 `All Subjects` *Reproducible*

TV Turnoff Week is a great week to do new things! Encourage students to provide suggestions of TV-free activities from the reproducible. FOR YOUNGER STUDENTS: Have them draw pictures of a favorite activity. FOR OLDER STUDENTS: Ask students to keep a journal of their week's choices of TV-free activities.

*Bulletin Board *Idea Decorate a bulletin board with a big TV with an X drawn through it. Attach students' drawings and best journal entries.

A TV-Free Community `Social Studies`

Get your school involved in TV Turnoff Week. Make posters and hang them all over school to announce the challenge and recruit volunteers. Make a big chart with names of volunteers and hang it in the hallway. Add an incentive: Throw a party at the end of the week with grab bag gifts (ask families to contribute) to celebrate TV-free efforts.

Earth Day/Arbor Day

April 22 (some states vary) • Worldwide

Earth Day is an ideal event for teaching the importance of nature, recycling, and conservation.

Holiday History *Read Aloud*

Did you know that Scholastic helped create the very first Earth Day in 1970? The first earth awareness holiday was Arbor Day, which started many years earlier. In the 1840s, pioneers who settled in a barren area of Nebraska recognized the need for trees. J. Sterling Morton, a journalist and pioneer, wrote in a Nebraska newspaper about the benefits of planting trees. The day became a legal holiday on April 22, Morton's birthday. *Scholastic NewsTime* Magazine published an article in 1969 announcing the idea of Earth Day to teachers and schoolchildren. Earth Day began the next year.

courtesy of Scholastic Inc.

Mark Your Calendar

Citizens across the country still plant trees on Arbor Day, but the date of the holiday varies from state to state. It's scheduled for when the local weather is most suitable for planting. For the Arbor Day date in your state, see The National Arbor Day Foundation's Web site at **www.arborday.org**.

Earth Day/Arbor Day

Fast Fact *Read Aloud*

Millions of plants and animals live in rain forests—more than half of the species on Earth! But rain forests are disappearing because people are cutting down the trees for wood and clearing the land for farming. Plants and animals are losing their homes as many countries lose their rain forests. About half of the world's rain forests are in South America. There are also rain forests in Central America, central Africa, and southeastern Asia.

~ Rain Forest ~
(sung to "I've Been Working on the Railroad")

I've been walking in the rain forest,
All among the trees.
I've been walking in the rain forest,
Where I saw the bats and bees.
Parrots, butterflies, and toucans,
Monkeys and hummingbirds galore.
Frogs and snakes and spotted leopards
On the rain forest floor!

I've been walking in the rain forest,
All among the green.
I've been walking in the rain forest,
Where the plant life must be seen!
Ferns and mosses and lianas,
Orchids and honeysuckle, too.
Oh, how special is the rain forest,
A magic place come true!

—from *101 Science Poems & Songs for Young Learners*

Bright Idea Reminder `Science`

Make hanging reminders of energy conservation. Students can write their own energy tips, or tips from the list below, on white cardboard cut in the shape of a lightbulb. Glue aluminum foil to the stem. Punch a hole at the top of the bulb shape, and thread a long piece of string through it. Tie the ends to create a loop for hanging. Urge students to take their reminders home and place them on the refrigerator, bathroom mirror, entertainment center, or any other spot in a high energy-usage area.

~ Save Energy ~

In cold weather . . .
- Make sure all doors are closed tightly.
- Wear warm clothes so you can keep the heat lower.
- Don't put large objects such as toys in front of radiators.
- Cover the bottom of doors where air comes in with a rug or door guard.

All year round . . .
- Always turn off the lights when you leave a room, and use natural daylight to light spaces.
- Don't open the refrigerator door more than you need to.
- Turn off the TV, computer, and electronic games when you're not using them.

—from Planet Pals Web site

★ Book Links

Lynne Cherry's travels to the Amazon rain forest come to life in her lush writings and illustrations. Her books include:

The Great Kapok Tree: A Tale of the Amazon Rain Forest (Harcourt, 1990). Picture book, all ages. A man begins to cut down a tree in the rain forest. While he sleeps, the animals explain how this act is destroying their world.

The Shaman's Apprentice: A Tale of the Amazon Rain Forest with Mark J. Plotkin (Harcourt, 1998). Picture book, intermediate. This true tale of a Tirio Indian boy tells a lesson about the importance of the rain forest plants.

Flute's Journey: The Life of a Wood Thrush (Harcourt, 1997). Picture book, intermediate. Cherry writes about the life of a wood thrush, from its hatching in a forest in Maryland to its migration to a Costa Rican rain forest.

★ Teacher Resource

101 Science Poems & Songs for Young Learners by Meish Goldish (Scholastic, 1996). For grades 1–3.

★ Web Link

The Planet Pals Web site at **www.planetpals.com** has handy tips on responsible energy conservation, plus school-oriented content such as lesson plans and a "teachers challenge."

Asian-Pacific Heritage Month

May 1–31 • United States

Study the heritage of Asian Americans during this month filled with holidays and traditions.

★ Book Links

The Name Jar by Yangsook Choi (Random House, 2001). Picture book, all ages. A girl named Unhei moves from Korea to the United States.

In the Year of the Boar and Jackie Robinson by Bette Bao Lord (HarperCollins, 1986). Chapter book, intermediate. This is the story of a Chinese immigrant girl named Shirley Temple Wong (her chosen name) in her first year in American public school, and how she gains strength from baseball's Jackie Robinson.

Baseball Saved Us by Ken Mochizuki (Lee & Low, 1995). Picture book, all ages. A baseball field gives courage to a Japanese-American family in a relocation camp during World War II.

★ Web Link

Find history, facts, and profiles on Asian Pacific Americans on the APAICS (Asian Pacific American Institute for Congressional Studies) Web site at **www.apaics.org/apa**.

Reproducible

Fast Fact ✦Read Aloud✦

There are many Asian Americans living in the United States today. They began settling here in the 1700s. Asian Americans have ancestors from many countries in the eastern hemisphere such as Japan, China, Hong Kong, Vietnam, Thailand, Singapore, India, Sri Lanka, Pakistan, and Bangladesh. Hawaiians are considered Pacific Islanders. Other Pacific Islanders live on tiny island countries that are hard to spot on a map including Fiji, the Cook Islands, and Solomon Islands—as well as hard-to-miss islands such as Australia.

✦Talk About It✦ Have you ever lived in or visited an Asian country? How was it different from and the same as where you live now?

Fast Fact

The attack on Pearl Harbor, on December 7, 1941, was one decisive event that caused the United States to enter World War II and declare Japan an enemy. Two months later, in February 1942, more than 120,000 Japanese Americans were taken to live in relocation camps in several western states. They were forced to leave their homes and jobs and live as prisoners for many months. This regrettable period in our history reminds us of the dangers of judging people because of their ethnicity.

In Other Words

Origami, translated from Japanese, means "folding" (ori) "paper" (gami). Asian Pacific countries have given us many useful and interesting words.

★ **ketchup:** from *kicap*, meaning "fish sauce" (Malay—Malaysia and Indonesia)

★ **chow:** means "food, miscellany" (Cantonese—southern China, Hong Kong)

★ **kung fu:** means "skill, art" (Mandarin—Beijing, China)

★ **boondocks:** from *bundok*, meaning "mountain" (Tagalog—northern Philippines)

★ **ukulele:** a small guitar, from words meaning "flea jumping" (Hawaii)

Origami Teacup, page 108 `Social Studies` `Math`

Origami, the Japanese art of paper folding, is a craft that's educational, too. Origami reinforces math skills—spatial reasoning, symmetry, and geometry. This reproducible shows how to make a simple cup.

Asian-Pacific Heritage Month

Fast Fact *Read Aloud*

The earliest recorded story of Cinderella comes from China. Yeh-Hsien is the ninth–century Chinese folk tale of a neglected young girl with an evil stepmother. The girl's fairy godmother is a magical fish that is her only friend. Other Asian countries also retell this story with an animal as its lead character:

★ **Philippines**: Mariango's fairy godmother, a crab, provides her with clothes and a carriage for the ball.

★ **Korea**: Kon-gy gets help from a frog and other animals to complete the tasks set by her stepmother. In this version, the glass slipper is a rubber shoe.

★ **India**: Godfather Snake has a magic jewel.

Fast Fact

The Chinese calendar is based on cycles of twelve years, with each year named after an animal. It is said that a person has certain traits of the animal he or she was born under.

Talk About It What's your Chinese animal sign? Does it reflect your personality?

Around the World

Here are some May holidays that center on the Asian family.

Japan: Boys' Festival (Tango-no-Sekku) On May 5, the Japanese dedicate a special day to boys. Traditionally, families with sons display *koi-nobori*, colorful fish banners with ribbons attached. One is hung on a bamboo pole outside the home (or miniature versions are hung inside) for each son in the family. The sizes differ depending on the sons' ages. The fish, a carp, is strong and brave because of its ability to swim upstream and leap up waterfalls. It symbolizes strength and success for the sons.

South Korea: Children's Day (Urini Nal) May 5 is the day parents recognize the respect that children pay them throughout the year. The day features many children's games. A popular contest is swinging high enough to hit a bell suspended in front of the swing. Many venues give free admission to children this day.

Korea: Parents' Day On May 8, Korean children honor their parents with gifts at family gatherings. Picnics feature contests in which children put a spin on kite flying: On the first hundred feet of string under the kite, they glue pieces of sharp ground glass. When kites cross in the air, the battle ends when a kite string is cut and the kite falls to the ground. Children race to capture the kite.

★ Book Links

Wishbones: A Folk Tale from China by Barbara Ker Wilson (Frances Lincoln, 1993). Picture book, all ages. A Chinese Cinderella story.

The Korean Cinderella by Shirley Climo (HarperCollins, 1993). Picture book, all ages. A classic Korean tale.

The Kite Fighters by Linda Sue Park (Dell, 2000). Chapter book, intermediate. Set in 1473, this timeless story tells of Korean brothers competing in a kite-fighting competition.

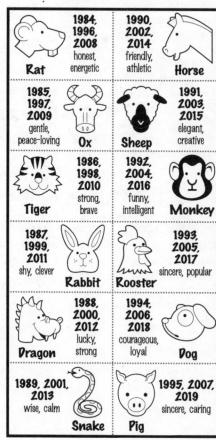

Rat 1984, 1996, 2008 honest, energetic		1990, 2002, 2014 friendly, athletic	**Horse**
Ox 1985, 1997, 2009 gentle, peace-loving		1991, 2003, 2015 elegant, creative	**Sheep**
Tiger 1986, 1998, 2010 strong, brave		1992, 2004, 2016 funny, intelligent	**Monkey**
Rabbit 1987, 1999, 2011 shy, clever		1993, 2005, 2017 sincere, popular	**Rooster**
Dragon 1988, 2000, 2012 lucky, strong		1994, 2006, 2018 courageous, loyal	**Dog**
Snake 1989, 2001, 2013 wise, calm		1995, 2007, 2019 sincere, caring	**Pig**

Physical Fitness and Sports Month

May 1–31 • United States

Many theories—the most famous of which is the Multiple Intelligences theory by Dr. Howard Gardner—suggest that certain people learn best by manipulating objects or physically completing a task. During this month devoted to physical fitness, put some movement into your lessons—and watch the results.

For more about the benefits of physical fitness, see Child Health Day in October on page 20.

★ Teacher Resources

Wiggle, Giggle and Shake: 200 Ways to Move and Learn by Rae Pica (Gryphon House, 2000). Pica introduces ways to incorporate movement into lessons. For younger students.

Getting More From Math Manipulatives by Birgitta Corneille (Scholastic, 1996). For grades K–2. Strategies, lessons, activities and assessment.

Sponge Relay   Math

Reinforce important math skills with this game that gets kids moving and thinking.

★ Take students to the playground and arrange them in teams. Set a bucket of water and a dry sponge at each team's start line. Set an empty bucket about 50 feet from the start (farther for older grades).

★ The first student in line dips the sponge into the bucket of water, runs to the empty bucket, and squeezes the water out of the sponge. The student runs back and passes the sponge to the next teammate.

★ After about five minutes, have students stop and measure the amount of liquid they've squeezed out of the sponges (they can use measuring cups to pour the collected water from the second bucket back into the emptied first bucket). The team with the most water in its bucket wins!

★ Let students read the markings on the measuring cup. Compare their results: Is $3/4$ cup greater or less than $1/2$ cup? Teams can write their results with greater than (>), less than (<), and equal (=) symbols.

National Postcard Week

Week of May 5 • United States

Everyone loves to get a postcard! Teach students about places around the world during this week that celebrates the beloved symbol of travel.

★ Book Link

Flat Stanley by Jeff Brown (HarperCollins, 1996). Picture book, all ages. A boy flattened to a half inch goes on geographic adventures.

Flying Freddy Travels the World, page 109   Social Studies   Language Arts

The Flat Stanley project, based on the book of the same name, has become famous in elementary schools around the country because it's an engaging way to teach about new places. Our reproducible features Flying Freddy. Ask families to send in a stamped envelope with the name and address of a friend or relative who lives far away. (Have stamps and envelopes on hand for students who forget. Ask the staff at your school to generate a list of trusted friends or contacts who would be willing to receive and respond to students' Freddy projects and assign those people to students who don't have a recipient for their Freddy.) Instructions are on the reproducible page.

Reproducible

*Bulletin Board *Idea   Display Flying Freddys and postcards against the backdrop of a world map on your bulletin board. Draw lines to connect postcards to their places of origin. Point to the location on the classroom map. Ask: Is this place north, south, east, or west of your home? What do you know about this place? What questions might you want to ask Flying Freddy about his adventure there?

May Day and Spring Festivals Around the World

May 1 (and throughout Spring) • United States, Europe, and other countries

May Day and other spring festivals shed light on the traditions of this season and its colorful bounty.

Holiday History
Many cultures around the world enjoy springtime festivals with traditions that date back hundreds of years. These celebrations recognize the coming of springtime and the planting season. The cold weather has left, and flowers begin to bloom—no wonder people feel like dancing in the sunshine! Learn about some traditions of spring festivals around the world below and on page 98. Use some or all of the party ideas to hold your own international spring festival.

Baswant ★ Northern India and Pakistan
Everyone wears yellow (*baswant* in Sanskrit) during this April spring festival. People fast in the morning and make offerings to Saraswati, the goddess of learning.

★Party! **Symbols of Springtime**: Ask students to wear their favorite springtime colors for a lesson on the symbols of the season: Yellow is for sunshine or sunflowers, green can be for grass, purple for orchids, white for lilies, and so on.

Holi ★ India/Hindu
Holi, held in late February/March, is a celebrated springtime festival in India. This is a true festival of color. Children enjoy smearing assorted powdered paints on each other, and they even fill bicycle pumps with colored water and squirt away! This tradition comes from a legend of the god Krishna, who on Holi played similar tricks on his companion Radha and her friends the *copis* (milkmaids).

★Party! **Seasonal Color Smearing**: Let students enjoy good old-fashioned finger painting on an old T-shirt with springtime hues like yellow and green. Use fabric paint that washes easily off hands. After the paint is dry, students can take their shirts home. (Send them with directions to place the shirts in a dryer for twenty minutes to set the color.)

Lei Day ★ Hawaii
Hawaii's May Day is Lei Day. On this day, everyone receives a lei—a large necklace laced with flowers— and a special greeting.

★Party! **Lei Craft**: Cut flowers (petals can be all shapes and sizes) out of colored tissue paper. Poke a tiny hole through the middle of each flower with a pin or a sharp pencil. Students can practice constructing patterns by lacing the flowers on a lanyard string interspersed with beads, buttons, tube-shaped pasta, and other treasures. Tie the string at top to fasten. Have students follow this tradition by exchanging leis and a high five.

Songkran ★ Thailand/Buddhist
Celebrated on April 13, Songkran is the celebration of springtime and the Thai New Year. Although the holiday is religious and serious, it also is a playful tribute to water. Traditional activities of water throwing and releasing fish into waterways symbolize rainfall and the hope for success in fishing.

May Day and Spring Festivals Around the World

May Day ★ Europe

When going "a-Maying," children in London trade flowers for pennies, which they throw into a wishing well. In France, parades feature cows with flowers tied on their tails. According to tradition, a person who touches one of the cows will have good luck! This custom dates back to the ancient traditions of Beltane, a Celtic festival during which people wore green leaves in their hats, danced outside, and lit bonfires to honor the Sun God. According to Beltane tradition, the cow and the bee were considered almost magical because of their plentiful production of milk and honey. Many Europeans enjoy the long-standing tradition of May Day: a ribbon dance around the maypole.

> **~ May Flowers ~**
> (to the tune of "The Mulberry Bush")
>
> Shout hurray for the flowers of May,
> Flowers of May, flowers of May.
> Shout hurray for the flowers of May,
> Pretty springtime flowers!
>
> Let's all play in the flowers of May,
> Flowers of May, flowers of May.
> Let's all play in the flowers of May,
> Pretty springtime flowers!
>
> —Jean Warren

★Party!

Flowers for Pennies: Have students make flower baskets—small mesh fruit containers with pipe-cleaner handles filled with paper flowers (see page 48 for easy tissue-paper flower instructions) and Easter basket grass. Give the flower baskets to teachers and staff in exchange for pennies, and donate the money to a local charity.

Cow and Bee Treat: To salute the sacred symbols of May Day, enjoy sweet products of the cow and bee: vanilla ice cream with honey.

Maypole Dance: Make your own maypole by decorating many long (and sturdy) ribbons or streamers with flowers and hanging them from a tall pole or tree. Each student holds a ribbon and skips around the pole. Traditionally, dancers wear bells to frighten away evil spirits.

Mayos ★ Spain

The Mayos, or Song Festival, is held from April 30 to May 3 to celebrate the rebirth of nature. Songs are sung about flowers and springtime.

★Party!

Songs of Spring: Sing "May Flowers," above. Students can make up springtime songs with their own lyrics and favorite traditional tunes.

Tu Bi-Shevat ★ Israel/Judaism

Held on the fifteenth day of Shevat in January or February, this holiday is the beginning of spring in Israel. Called the Trees' New Year, it is a time when schoolchildren plant trees.

★Party!

Plant a Tree: Make it an annual tradition to plant one tree or seedling on your school grounds or in a local park (you'll need official permission). Invite a local horticulturist or arborist to talk about trees and the environment. Incorporate this ritual with your Arbor Day celebration (see pages 92–93).

Cinco de Mayo

May 5 • Mexicans worldwide

Cinco de Mayo celebrates a free and unifed Mexico. It is a festive occasion to reintroduce lessons about Hispanic cultures.

In Other Words

Cinco de Mayo is Spanish for the "fifth of May." On this day in 1862, Mexican soldiers successfully fought off a French army three times its size to hold two important forts in Puebla de Los Angeles, Mexico. Though Mexico eventually lost the war, the Battle of Puebla is known as a turning point in Mexican patriotism. The increasing unity among the people of Mexico and their resistance toward foreign rule helped force the French out of Mexico by 1867.

America Celebrates

Cinco de Mayo has become a symbolic day of friendship between Mexicans and Mexican Americans. In Los Angeles, half a million people take part in the celebration. Along the streets—colored red, white, and green for Mexico's flag—come the sounds of traditional guitar and patriotic tunes, with dancers in authentic dress spinning and clicking away on their castanets. Picnics in city parks feature delicious Mexican foods.

> The month of September is Hispanic Heritage Month, which commemorates the official date of Mexico's independence from Spain on September 16, 1821. See pages 15–16.

★ Teacher Resource

Culture Kit: Mexico by Linda Scher and Mary Oates Johnson (Scholastic, 1995). For grades 1–4. Activities, projects, poster, audiotape, and map.

¡Fiesta! `Social Studies` `Art`

Put together a quick Mexican party to celebrate Cinco de Mayo.

★ **Tile Craft:** Create tiles like the famed Talavera tiles from the city of Puebla. Sketch simple designs on five-inch-square pieces of white construction paper. Add color by cutting and gluing pieces of tissue paper to the construction paper.

★ **Traditional Snacks:** Enjoy tortilla chips and salsa and *agua frescas*—juice made out of fresh fruit like watermelon, pineapple, or cantaloupe.

★ **Mexican Hat Dance:** Throw the sombrero, or any hat, in the middle of a circle of students, and dance! Point your right foot out—toe pointed up with the heel down—then switch feet with a quick hop. The familiar song goes like this: Da DUM da DUM da DUM! (clap clap) Da DEEDLE dee DUM da DUM! (clap clap) (repeat). Hop at every beat (words in caps)—so you switch feet three times, clap twice, and repeat.

In Other Words

No Mexican hat dance is complete without a *sombrero*. A traditional sombrero has a wide brim and is made of straw.

~ Cinco de Mayo ~
(to the tune of "La Cucaracha")

Cinco de Mayo, Cinco de Mayo
Mexico's Independence Day
Cinco de Mayo, Cinco de Mayo
It is the day to say, "Hurray!"

The French invaded the town of Puebla
In the year 1862
Zaragoza, he was the leader
His soldiers fought so brave and true.

The forts in Puebla, they were important
And the army was so small
But they defeated the large French army—
The greatest battle of them all.

Cinco de Mayo, Cinco de Mayo
Let's all sing and shout, "Olé!"
Cinco de Mayo, Cinco de Mayo
Happy Independence Day!

Mother's Day

Second Sunday in May • United States, France, Sweden (last Sunday in May), and other countries

Mother's Day is celebrated around the world to pay tribute to the mother figures in our lives. Share lessons of caring and giving, and enjoy projects with mom in mind.

Every family is different—and special. For thoughts on how to approach all students during this family-oriented holiday, see the "Father . . . or father figure?" box on page 114.

★ Book Links

A Gift for Mama by Esther Hautzig (Penguin, 1981). Chapter book, intermediate. A Jewish girl in Poland decides to buy a gift for her mother.

Holiday History *Read Aloud*

Mother's Day became a national holiday in the United States in 1914 after Anna Jarvis from Philadelphia, Pennsylvania, campaigned to create a special day to honor all mothers. But the idea for a day to pay tribute to mothers wasn't new. In ancient Greece, people celebrated Rhea, the mother of six important gods and goddesses. In Rome, she was called Cybele. In England, Mothering Sunday was a holiday for Christians to visit the church where they were baptized.

Mom Acrostic (Language Arts)

Have students make up new words to the song at right with acrostic verses that describe their special feelings; for example: "'M' is for the million books you read me." Help them brainstorm the special moments they've shared with their mothers. Students can include the verses in a special card to send home.

~ M-O-T-H-E-R~

"M" is for the million things she gave me,

"O" means only that she's growing old,

"T" is for the tears she shed to save me,

"H" is for her heart of purest gold;

"E" is for her eyes, with love-light shining,

"R" means right, and right she'll always be,

Put them all together, they spell "MOTHER,"

A word that means the world to me.

—Howard Johnson (circa 1915)

Mark Your Calendar

Schedule the Friday before Mother's Day as a day to welcome moms and other special female caregivers to lead the class in a special activity—reading a book, making a craft, or playing a game.

Mother, May I? (All Subjects)

Try this game of "Mother, May I?" with an educational twist. Have students remain in their seats; divide class into two teams. Alternating teams, Mother asks a student to stand. Mother then asks that student a math, spelling, or any grade-appropriate question: "What is 3 + 4?" "Spell the word *artwork*." "Who wrote *Charlotte's Web*?" (You can prepare a sheet of questions in advance.) The student then asks, "Mother, May I?" If the response is "Yes, you may," the student must answer correctly. A correct answer earns a point for the team; an incorrect answer gets no points. The winning team gets a special treat from Mother!

Mother's Day Favorites Venn Diagram, page 110 (Language Arts)

Have students interview their moms or any special mother figure in their lives using the list of favorites on the reproducible. They can compare and contrast their mom's likes and dislikes with their own by using the overlapping area of the heart shapes to show the favorite things they have in common, and the "mom" and "me" sections to show the differences they have. FOR OLDER STUDENTS: Invite students to use the information they gathered in their interview to write a short descriptive piece. This can be used as a caption for a portrait they draw of their mother.

Reproducible

Memorial Day

Last Monday in May • United States

Introduce students to this important holiday that commemorates those who died to preserve the freedom of the United States.

Holiday History

Memorial Day was inaugurated in 1868 by General John Logan after the Civil War, which had ended three years earlier. Through time, and more war, it has become a day of tribute to all of our nation's heroic soldiers who have lost their lives in combat.

In Other Words

Memorial Day was originally called Decoration Day because it was established as the day to decorate or honor the graves of fallen soldiers.

Signs of Peace Language Arts

Urge students to talk about what they know about past wars and times of peace and justice. Continue this discussion by sharing the words of great writers, artists, and poets. Let students look for famous passages written in *Barlett's Familiar Quotations* or on **www.poets.org** (search by key words such as "war" and "peace"). Students should write the poems they've selected on the left side of a piece of 8¹/₂- by 11-inch piece of white paper, held horizontally. (While older students can copy the poems in their best cursive, you may need to write out the poems for younger students.) Then, to the right of each poem, have students draw a symbol for the poem. For example, they might trace their hand making a peace sign (fingers tucked into a fist with index and middle finger extended in the shape of a "V"). Encourage students to decorate in patriotic colors and write their own peace slogan below.

★Talk About ★It What do the words *war*, *peace*, and *justice* mean in these quotations (at right)? What do they mean to you?

For more about celebrating war veterans, see Veterans Day in November on page 32.

★ Teacher Resources

Education World features a lesson on Memorial Day at **www.education-world.com**. Click on Holidays in the Reference Center for all holiday materials. The site also includes links.

Bartlett's Familiar Quotations, 17th Edition (Little, Brown & Company, 2002). Quotations, poetry, prose, and more from across the centuries. Listed by author and thematic key word.

~ EXCERPTS ~

The purpose of all war is peace.
—Saint Augustine, Algerian bishop (354–430)

Peace is more important than all justice; and peace was not made for the sake of justice, but justice for the sake of peace.
—Martin Luther, German theologian (1483–1546)

When we say "War is over if you want it," we mean that if everyone demanded peace instead of another TV set, we'd have peace.
—John Lennon, musician (1940–1980)

Memorial Day

Memorial Day Fact Hunt `Social Studies` `Language Arts`

Challenge students to use the Internet to research the meaning of Memorial Day with a scavenger hunt. Tasks might include:

★ reading historic U.S. documents that show what American soldiers fought and died for.

★ researching and writing biographies on women veterans such as Revolutionary War hero Molly Pitcher.

★ researching memorials like "The Wall," the Vietnam Veterans Memorial in Washington, D.C.

★ discussing war propaganda posters.

★ learning about the proper way to fold a flag.

Traditions Today *Read Aloud*

Memorial Day is a national holiday. Schools and businesses are closed. Across the country, flags fly at half-mast—they are drawn only halfway up the flagpole. Many towns have parades and special ceremonies to honor the fallen soldiers and their families. Traditions include a soldier playing "Taps" on a bugle as a wreath is placed on a memorial site.

America Celebrates

Most U.S. towns celebrate Memorial Day with a parade featuring a marching band and local veterans, ending with a solemn ceremony to remember the hometown heroes who died in combat. At Arlington National Cemetery in Virginia, outside Washington, D.C., important government officials attend a ceremony at the Tomb of the Unknowns, where one soldier from both world wars and from the Korean and Vietnam wars are buried. The tomb represents all soldiers in all wars.

★Talk About ★It — How does our town commemorate fallen soldiers? (Note: Students may have loved ones who are on active duty in the military. They may need to share their stories and feel the support of the class community.)

Fast Fact

By Congressional rule adopted in 1942, the United States requires that a flag at half-mast is flown exactly halfway between the top and bottom of the flagstaff. Some countries still follow the old naval tradition where a flag is lowered one flag's width below the top of the pole, leaving space for an invisible flag to fly above it. This invisible flag represents the person who is deceased.

Name _____

Date _____

Famous Women in History Mobiles

Create a fact mobile about an important woman in history. Here's how!

Draw a picture of the woman's face on a small paper plate (or round piece of construction paper) and decorate it with yarn or ribbon for hair. Glue or tape the face to the hook of a hanger. Write your facts in the shapes below and cut them out. Poke a hole at the top of each shape; attach a 12-inch piece of ribbon or yarn. Tie each ribbon to the hanger so that the shapes dangle.

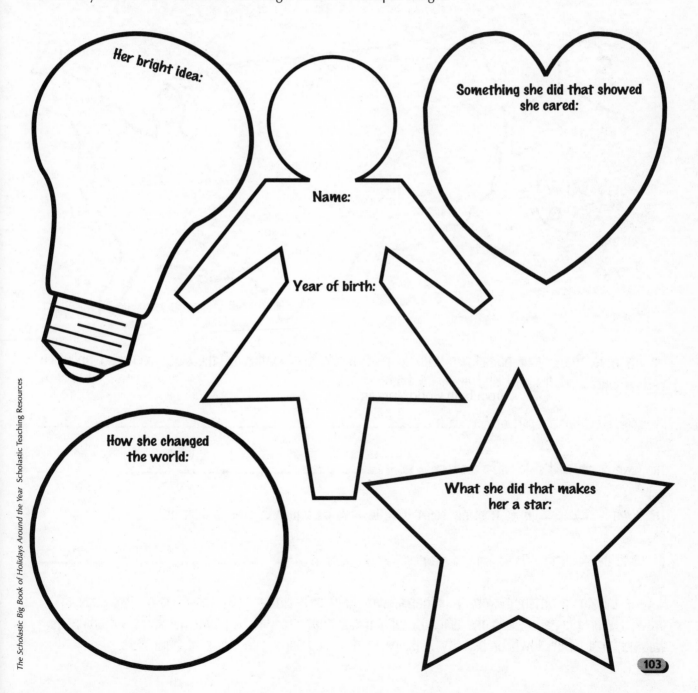

Her bright idea:

Something she did that showed she cared:

Name:

Year of birth:

How she changed the world:

What she did that makes her a star:

Read Across America

Books From Across America

You know your hometown. What do you know about the town or city in the book you just read? Answer these questions to find out!

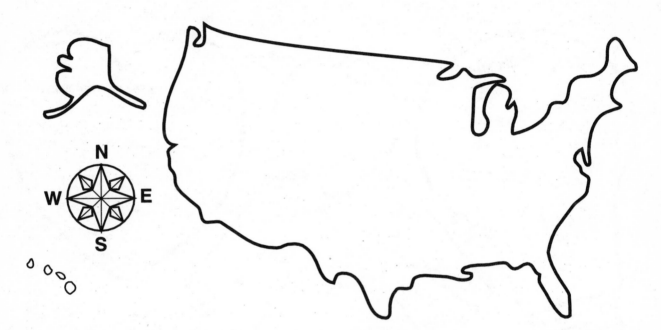

On the map, mark your hometown with a heart. Mark the location of the place you read about with a star. Label the city and state for both.

My book about another part of America is _____

The town or city and state where the book is set is _____

This town is _____ miles from my home. (Use the scale on a map or atlas to estimate.)

To get to this town from my town, the direction I would travel is _____

How is this town different from your hometown? How is it similar? Use the back of this page to draw a Venn diagram. Fill in the diagram with things that are different and the same, including the weather, size (small town or big city?), things to do, geography, and types of businesses.

The Scholastic Big Book of Holidays Around the Year Scholastic Teaching Resources

Name _____

Date _____

My Day at Work

What is your workday like? You, or a supervising adult, can make notes on this page.
Tell your class all about it tomorrow!

I went to work with _____.

My _____ works for _____ (name of business).

This business _____ (what the business does).

My _____'s day at work is filled with responsibilities like _____,
_____, and _____ (what the person does at the business).

My _____'s favorite part of the job is _____.

This is what I did at work today. (Write down your activities below. Draw the time by adding the
hour hand and minute hand on the clocks.)

At _____, we _____
_____.

At _____, we _____
_____.

At _____, we _____
_____.

At _____, we _____
_____.

I think this job is a good match for my skills and interests: YES or NO. (circle one)

When I grow up, I would like to be _____.

National Coin Week

State Quarter Fact Sheet

What do you know about New York, Virginia, and other states? Let the state quarters help! Answer these questions about one state quarter and share what you've learned with your class.

Draw or do a pencil rubbing in these circles.

Front of quarter

Back of quarter

This state quarter represents _____ (state's name).

The capital of this state is _____ .

This state was the _____ state to join the United States.

The symbol on the back of this state quarter is _____ .

This symbol is important to the state because _____

_____ .

Three facts I learned about this state are:

★ _____ .

★ _____ .

★ _____ .

Name _____

Date _____

TV Turnoff Week

My Week Without TV

After the TV goes off, what do you do? Here are a few brain-boosting alternatives!

 Straighten your home book collection. Put books in order by author or by subject (super-heroes, animals, and so on). Weed out books you don't read anymore. Have a book exchange with friends.

 Clean your sock drawer. Pair matching socks. Make puppets out of single socks. (Sew or glue on stray buttons for eyes.) Hold a puppet show!

 Roll up spare change: 50 pennies in a roll ($.50), 20 nickels in a roll ($1), 50 dimes in a roll ($5), 40 quarters in a roll ($10). Cash the rolls in at your local bank and save the cash for a rainy day or donate it to a local charity!

 Look at all of your board games. Make necessary repairs. If pieces are missing, find—or make—new pieces. Write a set of new rules. Then play the games you fixed up!

 Clean out the refrigerator. Pour any old food into a big pot in the sink. (Stay away from moldy foods, and don't taste!) See what happens when you add heavy items such as baking soda or salt, and dark-colored liquids.

 Have a toy sale in which every item is $.50. Make receipts for the customers.

 Make your old toys like new. Wash plastic toys in a wading pool or sink with a little dish detergent. Pretend it's the ocean, and have an underwater adventure!

BONUS: Keep a journal during TV Turnoff Week.

On Monday, instead of watching TV, I _____ .

On Tuesday, instead of watching TV, I _____ .

On Wednesday, instead of watching TV, I _____ .

On Thursday, instead of watching TV, I _____ .

On Friday and all weekend, instead of watching TV, I _____ .

Asian-Pacific Heritage Month

Origami Teacup

Make a teacup using the Japanese art of paper folding called origami. Decorate the square below and cut it out. Follow the directions below for folding the square. Have a tea party!

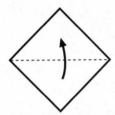

(A) Fold to make a triangle (decorated side faces away from you).

(B) Fold points across, as shown (folds make congruent triangles, points overlap slightly).

(C) Fold top flaps down— one to the front, one to the back.

(D) Puff out sides to make the cup.

Flying Freddy Travels the World

This is Flying Freddy. He wants to visit your town. Would you take him around with you for a day? Please send me a postcard describing the things you did together as soon as you can! Thank you.

Signed, _____

Flying Freddy wants to go on an adventure. Decorate Freddy, and then cut him out. Make sure to sign your name! Now put Freddy inside a stamped envelope addressed to a friend or relative who lives in a unique or faraway place. Bring it to school tomorrow for mailing. When your postcard arrives, bring it in right away to show your class!

Mother's Day

Name _____

Date _____

Mother's Day Favorites Venn Diagram

What's the mom in your life really like? Find out about some of her favorite things and write them down below. Compare them to your own! Hint: Here are some favorites to compare: colors, hobbies, books, songs, vacation places, rooms in your home, activites you do together, flowers or trees, snack foods.

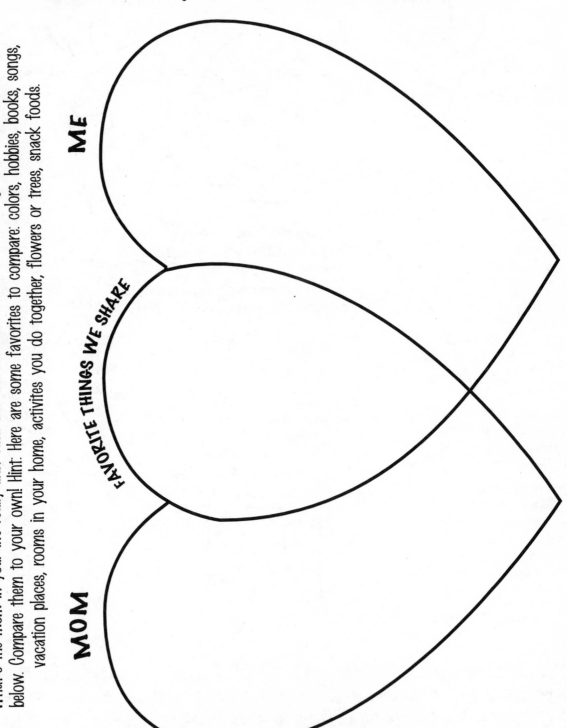

ME

MOM

FAVORITE THINGS WE SHARE

The Scholastic Big Book of Holidays Around the Year Scholastic Teaching Resources

Summer Calendar
June

June 14	FLAG DAY	United States	112
Third Sunday in June	FATHER'S DAY	United States and other countries	114
June 21 or 22	SUMMER SOLSTICE	Worldwide	115
June 27	HAPPY BIRTHDAY'S BIRTHDAY and BIRTHDAY CELEBRATIONS AROUND THE WORLD	Worldwide	117

July

| July 4 | INDEPENDENCE DAY (Fourth of July) | United States | 119 |
| July 24 | MORMON PIONEER DAY | Mormon | 121 |

August

| August or September | KRISHNA JANMASTAMI | Hindu | 121 |
| August 1–31 | NATIONAL INVENTORS MONTH | United States | 122 |

Do you have some extra time for holiday celebration this summer?
Try celebrating Kwanzaa in July and Native American Indian Heritage Month in August!
Let students help choose a holiday you might have missed during the year.
Enjoy the new tradition!

 **Summer Reproducibles**

Flag Day:
A Special Flag 123

Father's Day:
Father's Day Find Out 124

Independence Day:
Special Words From the Declaration of Independence 125

 For great ideas for celebrating students' birthdays, see Birthday Celebrations Around the World in June on pages 117–118.

Flag Day

June 14 • United States (American Samoa—April 17)

On this day of tribute to our flag, teach about this important American symbol and its heritage.

Holiday History *Read Aloud*

On June 14, 1777, less than a year after the signing of the Declaration of Independence and the birth of the United States, the American flag was raised for the first time. The idea of a "flag birthday" came from Wisconsin public school teacher B. J. Cigrant in 1885. Word of Flag Day slowly spread to New York City, then to Philadelphia and Chicago, until it was proclaimed an official national holiday by President Truman in 1949.

Fast Fact *Read Aloud*

The design of the American flag has special meaning. There are thirteen red and white stripes to represent the thirteen original colonies. One theory states that the red stripes represent England and the white stripes represent the United States, and that they alternate to show our independence. President Taft established the official pattern of the stars in 1912. The white stars on the blue background represent each of the states in the Union.

America Celebrates

Elizabeth ("Betsy") Griscom Ross was an upholstery shop owner in Philadelphia during the American Revolution. As the story goes, General George Washington appeared at her door in June of 1776 with a sketch of the flag for the new country, and Ross agreed to sew it.

Fast Fact *Read Aloud*

The American flag you might hang outside your door or window typically measures 3 by 5 feet. A flag flying on a pole at your school might be slightly bigger: 4 by 6 feet. Ever wonder how big the biggest American flag is? It's called "Superflag" and it's the size of three football fields!

A Five-Pointed Star Social Studies

Make the five-pointed star, most likely invented by Betsy Ross for the first flag of the United States of America.

★ Cut off 1 inch from the bottom of an 8½- by 11-inch sheet of paper to make it 8½- by 10 inches.

★ Fold the paper in half. Write the letters A, B, and C as shown.

★ Fold corner A to B. Mark the new corner D.

★ Fold corner C over the paper edge running from B to D (see dotted line in diagram).

★ Fold this heartlike shape in half to make a cone shape.

★ Cut the paper as shown. Unfold the star.

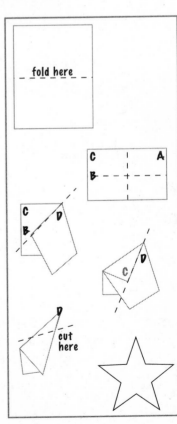

Flag Day

A Special Flag, page 123 `Social Studies`

The colors on the American flag were chosen specifically because they symbolize important ideas about our country's fight for freedom. Help students learn about the colors—and have some patriotic fun—by reading the poem on the reproducible and discussing the meanings of the descriptive words listed for each color.

Reproducible

★ Book Link

The Star-Spangled Banner illustrated by Peter Spier (Random House, 1973). Picture book, all ages. This illustrated version of the anthem includes pictures of American flags throughout history.

Fast Fact *Read Aloud*

The American flag is the only flag to be featured in its country's national anthem. Francis Scott Key, a lawyer, wrote the poem in 1814. He was inspired by the sight of a flag flying at Fort McHenry in Maryland after a fierce battle against the British during the War of 1812.

> ### ~ The Star-Spangled Banner ~
>
> Oh, say can you see
> By the dawn's early light
> What so proudly we hail'd
> At the twilight's last gleaming?
> Whose broad stripes and bright stars
> Through the perilous fight
> O'er the ramparts we watch'd
> Were so gallantly streaming?
>
> And the rockets' red glare,
> The bombs bursting in air,
> Gave proof through the night
> That our flag was still there.
> Oh, say does that star-spangled banner yet wave
> O'er the land of the free
> And the home of the brave?
> —Francis Scott Key (1814)

Holiday History *Read Aloud*

Where did the Pledge of Allegiance come from? On October 12, 1892, a Boston magazine called *The Youth's Companion* waged a campaign for students across the country to read a special passage to celebrate the 400th anniversary of Columbus's discovery of America. More than 12 million students recited the Pledge of Allegiance that day, beginning the important ritual that continues today.

★Talk About ★It The words "under God" were added to the Pledge of Allegiance in 1954 by President Eisenhower to affirm "religious faith in America's heritage and future." Why might some people object to the addition of that phrase to the pledge?

> ### The Pledge ~ of Allegiance ~
>
> I pledge allegiance
> To the flag
> Of the United States of America,
> And to the republic
> For which it stands,
> One nation under God,
> Indivisible,
> With liberty and justice for all.

Father's Day

Third Sunday in June • United States and other countries

This is the official day to recognize Dad in a celebration of family and relationships.

Father . . . or father figure? A student's parents might not be his or her birth parents. There may be another caretaker who is equally special. During holidays such as Father's Day and Mother's Day, use terms such as "the special adult who cares for you" or "the mom or dad in your life" to help all students feel included.

★ Book Link

Owl Moon by Jane Yolen, illustrated by John Schoenherr (Putnam, 1987). Picture book, all ages. A father and daughter's exploration to see the great horned owl describes a warm parent-child relationship.

Holiday History *Read Aloud*

Father's Day became a legal holiday in our country in 1972. The tradition began on June 19, 1910, when Sonora Smart Dodd from Spokane, Washington, started a petition to recognize the hard work of fathers. Dodd's mother had died when she was young, and her father had raised her and her five brothers and sisters by himself. Dodd had heard about Mother's Day, which was a new holiday then, and thought there should be a special day to honor fathers, too.

Talk About It (See excerpt.) How is your father (or the special man who cares for you, such as your grandfather, older brother, or uncle) like a teacher?

~ EXCERPT ~
One father is more than a hundred schoolmasters.
—English proverb

Reproducible

Father's Day Find Out, page 124 `Language Arts`

Try this conversation starter about the importance of fathers in students' lives. Distribute copies of the reproducible and ask students to fill out the web with information about their lives and their special relationship with a father figure. Invite students to present their finished information webs to the class. FOR OLDER STUDENTS: Urge students to bring in current pictures and stories of these father figures as well as pictures of them as children and young men. (To protect the photos, suggest that students store them in resealable plastic sandwich bags.) Ask them to tape each picture to the top of a sheet of construction paper, design a frame, and write a caption based on the information they gathered using their web.

Father's Day Tie `Social Studies`

A popular gift for that special guy is a tie. This tie will be a special keepsake that he'll treasure.

★ Ask students to bring in old cloth ties in solid colors. If a cloth tie is unavailable, cut scrap fabric or construction paper into the shape of a tie.

★ Ask students to paint their cloth ties with fabric paint or color their paper ties with markers.

★ After the paint has dried, have each student cut out a family picture and glue it in the middle of the tie. Students who do not have pictures can draw a portrait of their father or create construction paper symbols to glue on.

Summer Solstice

June 21 or 22 • Northern hemisphere

Welcome the beginning of summer with lessons on Earth's revolution around the sun, and how the sun has been honored throughout history.

Fast Fact *Read Aloud*

The summer solstice is the longest day of the year. The sun is farthest away from Earth's equator, so there are more hours of daylight. In the northern hemisphere (the part of the world north of or above the equator), the summer solstice occurs each year on June 21 or 22. In the southern hemisphere (the part of the world south of or below the equator), this date is the winter solstice, and it is the shortest day of the year (see page 48).

Northern Hemisphere

Southern Hemisphere

★ Book Link

Arrow to the Sun: A Pueblo Indian Tale by Gerald McDermott (Penguin Putnam, 1974). Picture book, all ages. An engaging story about the Dance of Life.

In Other Words

Solstice comes from the Latin words meaning "sun stands still."

More Daylight! `Science`

Perform this light demonstration with a big ball (like a beach ball) and a flashlight. Turn off the lights in the classroom. Hold the flashlight (sun) very close to the ball (Earth) and show how Earth revolves around the sun. A student helper with the flashlight can stand in place and turn, following the ball with the flashlight beam while you walk around him or her and spin the ball to show how night and day happen. Now rotate the ball so that the bottom of the ball faces the light. Point out that one half or hemisphere is now receiving more daylight (summer solstice) while the other hemisphere is mostly in darkness (winter solstice). This process is reversed six months later when the hemisphere that was facing the sun now faces away and experiences winter solstice while the hemisphere that was mostly in darkness now receives increased daylight.

America Celebrates

The Sun Dance Ceremony was the most important religious ceremony of the nineteenth-century Plains Indians, which included the Arapaho, Cheyenne, Sioux, and Omaha tribes. Beginning during the summer solstice or soon after, the ceremony lasted four to eight days. An important symbol of the ceremony was a sunpole, a tree believed to connect Earth to heaven. The rituals exemplified Native Americans' beliefs that there is no true end to life and that elements of nature are reliant upon one another. For more about the celebration of Native American traditions, see National American Indian Heritage Month in November on pages 29–30.

Traditions Today

Summer is a great celebration for everyone around the world. Great Britain and other European countries celebrate the solstice on June 24 on the Christian holiday St. John's Eve, which honors the death of John the Baptist. People in Nordic countries like Denmark, Sweden, and Norway call the holiday Midsummer's Eve (a misnomer, since it is the beginning of summer). They enjoy ancient rituals such as bonfires and circle dances (see page 116).

Summer Solstice

Circle Dances Social Studies

Lead your class in these two dances that celebrate the solstice. Play soft New Age music in the background.

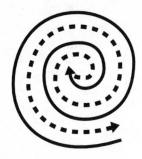

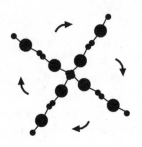

Spiral Dance

In this dance, the center of the circle represents the sun, which ancient druids believed to be the source of all life.

★ Dancers face each other in a circle and hold hands. The circle begins to move in one direction. Urge the dancers to move their bodies to the beat.

★ One dancer is the leader. At any given time, the leader lets go of the hand of the person in front of him or her and walks past that person on the inside, leading the line around and around in a spiral until he or she reaches the center of the circle. (Everyone else continues to hold hands.)

★ The leader then turns around and walks out of the spiral by going between the two rows of people who are moving inward. If everyone holds hands throughout the dance, the group will end up back in a circle that is facing outward!

★TIP★ It's best to have a teacher lead the spiral dance because younger students tend to go too fast. Remind them to continue holding hands and move at a medium pace to avoid yanking and pulling one another.

Wheel Dance

The turning of the wheel symbolizes the changing of the seasons.

★ Four students form a circle, and join right hands. They are the center spokes of the wheel. Other students join the wheel with their right hands holding the left hands of the students who are the center spokes. Another group of four students can add a ring to the circle by joining their right hands to the left hands of the last group. Continue to add groups of four students or begin a new wheel.

★ Direct students to move a step forward to "spin" the wheel clockwise. The spinning movement symbolizes the changing of the seasons. After several rotations, stop the dance and have the first four students in the center let go and move to the outside of the wheel. The students who were holding their left hands will move to the center and form a new set of center spokes.

★ Continue to spin the wheel until every student has a turn in the center.

Happy Birthday's Birthday

June 27 • Worldwide

"Happy Birthday to You . . ." **Celebrate the birthday of the famous song by sharing some educational and entertaining birthday traditions from around the world.**

Holiday History *Read Aloud*

The song "Happy Birthday to You" was born on June 27, 1859, when sisters and schoolteachers Mildred Hill and Dr. Patty Smith Hill of Louisville, Kentucky, wrote the song for their students. Mildred composed the music, which was first published with Patty's lyrics as a classroom greeting song called "Good Morning to All."

> Because of the beliefs of certain religions and cultures, some students might not celebrate birthdays. For more information, see page 7.

Fast Fact *Read Aloud*

The tradition of birthday parties started in Europe a long time ago, but the parties weren't celebrations. People feared that evil spirits were especially attracted to them at a time of a change in their lives such as a birthday. To protect the birthday person from harm, friends and family visited and surrounded him or her with laughter, joy, and best wishes, to keep away the evil spirits. Gifts protected the person even more.

Birthday Celebrations Around the World

Here are some special traditions that show how families around the world celebrate birthdays.

Announcing a Birthday

United States: Americans often hang balloons outside the front door to show that there's a birthday boy or girl inside.

Denmark: Danish people fly their country's flag outside their homes to signify that someone in the family is having a birthday.

Philippines: Filipino families display blinking colored lights to show that someone is celebrating a birthday.

Celebrating the Birthday Boy or Girl

United States: While the partygoers sing "Happy Birthday," they present the birthday boy or girl with a cake with lit candles. The child makes a wish. If he or she blows out all the candles on the cake, it is believed that the wish will come true.

Argentina: Have students ever gotten a pinch to grow an inch? Argentine children get a pull on their earlobe—one for each year of their life.

Ireland: An Irish child gets "birthday bumps." He or she is held upside down and is bumped on the floor—once for each year and once more for good luck.

Israel: An Israeli birthday child wears a crown of flowers. He or she sits in a special chair, which is lifted in the air—once for each year with an extra lift for luck.

Norway: In school, the birthday child dances in front of the class with a friend while the other students sing a birthday song.

Happy Birthday's Birthday

★ Book Links

Henry's First-Moon Birthday by Lenore Look (Simon & Schuster, 2001). Picture book, all ages. A Chinese girl prepares for her brother's first-moon (one month) birthday party.

Celebrating a Quiñceanera: A Latina's Fifteenth Birthday Celebration by Diane Hoyt-Goldsmith (Holiday House, 2002). Picture book, intermediate. This photo essay follows Mexican-American girl Cynthia Cuevas and the rituals leading up to her 15th birthday celebration.

Foods and Feasts

United States: American children eat birthday cakes that have special messages written in icing.

England: Some English birthday cakes are baked with small figures and fake coins inside. This is an old tradition from medieval times when people believed that finding a coin in a piece of cake meant they would become rich.

China: Chinese families serve special noodles for lunch to honor the birthday child. They are extra–long to symbolize a long life.

Russia: Russian children get birthday pies instead of cakes. Similar to American cake, the pie is inscribed with a message carved into the crust.

Sweden: A Swedish birthday child gets breakfast in bed!

The Most Special Birthdays

United States: While all birthdays are special for American children, a girl's sweet sixteen is a notable day.

China: The first-moon birthday occurs at the end of the child's first month of life. This party is a great celebration. One of the traditions is dying eggs red for good luck.

Netherlands: Even-numbered birthday years are called crown years. On these birthdays, children get especially large gifts.

Egypt: An Egyptian child's first birthday is very important. Flowers and fruit decorate the party room, symbolizing life and growth.

Japan: A child's third, fifth, and seventh birthdays are thought to be especially lucky. Every November 15, their birthdays are celebrated during the *Shichi-go-san* (Seven-five-three) festival. On this day, children who turned seven, five, or three that year wear their best clothes and receive special gifts.

Korea: The *Baek-il* is the 100th day after a child is born. Families feast on symbolic Korean foods to wish the child safety and a good life. *Tol* is the child's first birthday. The highlight is *Toljabee*, an event in which the child picks items off a table that will predict the future. If the child picks a book, he or she will become a scholar. If the child picks a rice cake, he or she will be rich.

Latin America: *Quinceañera* is a girl's fifteenth birthday. This marks her passage into adulthood and is celebrated with a huge party.

Religious Birthday Traditions

Hindu: According to custom, Hindu children do not celebrate birthdays until they are sixteen years old. Until that year, they cannot attend school on their birthdays.

Jewish: Jewish boys and girls are considered adults when they are thirteen and twelve, respectively. A bar mitzvah for boys and a bat mitzvah for girls is a celebration welcoming him or her into the adult community. (Note: Bar and bat mitzvahs can, but usually do not, occur on the birthday.)

Muslim: When a Muslim baby is one week old, the family holds a ceremony where the child's head is shaved. The family donates money to the poor equal to the weight of the child's hair.

Independence Day (Fourth of July)

July 4 • United States

Celebrate America's freedom with lessons about our history and heritage.

Holiday History *Read Aloud*

July 4, 1776, is the day the United States was born. Before then, the British ruled the American colonies. The colonists—people who came from Britain to settle in America's thirteen colonies—were unhappy with the way they were treated by the British. They wanted the freedom to make their own rules and live without answering to the king of England. General George Washington led the colonists in a war against the British, and won. On this day, our forefathers signed the Declaration of Independence, which announced our freedom from British rule.

In Other Words

At one time, many modern countries were territories owned by other countries. Just like the United States, the people of these places decided that they wanted to establish their own countries. The date of the independence holiday usually marks the day in history when freedom was officially won. Many countries call the holiday Independence Day. Independence means being free of something or someone. Others name it for the founding of the new nation or republic, calling it National Day, Republic Day, Founders Day, or they name the day for the country itself like Canada Day. Still others cite a famous battle, like France's Bastille Day.

Special Words from the Declaration of Independence, page 124 (Social Studies) (Language Arts)

Reproducible

The famous words from our Declaration of Independence excerpted at right capture the essence of the freedom the colonists fought to win. Discuss the meaning of the passage, especially these words and phrases: *equal*; *Rights*; *Life, Liberty and the pursuit of Happiness*. Have students write down what these words mean to them and use one of the words (or another word from the document) in a special bumper sticker. FOR YOUNGER STUDENTS: Let students draw pictures of Americans enjoying their rights as citizens.

Show your patriotism by celebrating our nation's great symbol, the American flag. For information and activities, see Flag Day in June on pages 112–113.

★ Book Links

If You Lived in the Time of the American Revolution by Kay Moore (Scholastic, 1998). Picture book, intermediate. Details about the American Revolution presented in an easy-to-read question-and-answer format.

The Declaration of Independence: The Words That Made America illustrated and inscribed by Sam Fink (Scholastic, 2002). Picture book, all ages. Fink's illustrations make the complicated words of the document accessible to all students.

~ EXCERPT ~

We hold these truths to be self-evident, that all men are created equal, that they are endowed by their Creator with certain unalienable Rights, that among these are Life, Liberty and the pursuit of Happiness.

—from the Declaration of Independence

Independence Day (Fourth of July)

★ Book Links

Yankee Doodle by Dr. Richard Shackburg, (Simon & Schuster, 1965). Picture book, all ages. The verses of this song were first sung during the Battle of Lexington.

Fireworks, Picnics, and Flags: The Story of Fourth of July Symbols by James Cross Giblin (Houghton Mifflin, 2001). Chapter book, intermediate. A tool for research on the history of Independence Day and its symbols, such as Uncle Sam and the bald eagle.

Fast Fact ⋆Read Aloud⋆

Did you know that the patriotic song "Yankee Doodle" isn't American at all? The words and music are from a fifteenth-century Dutch harvesting song that began, "Yanker dudel doodle down." The British created many renditions of the song, one of which makes fun of the colonists in the Revolution. The colonists, however, adopted "Yankee Doodle" as their battle cry and it remains an all-American tune today. In fact, it's the official song of the state of Connecticut.

~ Yankee Doodle ~

Yankee Doodle went to town,
A-riding on a pony,
Stuck a feather in his hat,
And called it macaroni.

Yankee Doodle keep it up,
Yankee Doodle dandy,
Mind the music and the step,
And with the girls be handy.

—Richard Shuckburgh,
British surgeon (circa 1755)

Independence Day Picnic `Social Studies`

Throw an Independence Day picnic. Sit near your school flagpole and sing patriotic songs. Make your own fife (kazoo) and drum (coffee can) band and march around to the tune of "Yankee Doodle." Share picnic snacks—ask families for contributions of red, white, and blue foods (e.g., strawberries, blueberries, and whipped cream).

Holiday History

The most colorful symbol of our Independence Day celebration is the fireworks display. Believe it or not, the first fireworks invented were white! The ancient Chinese lit up their night skies in celebration with white light, using the same technology as the first rocket. The British brought fireworks to America in the early seventeenth century, and within the next 200 years they burst with color. Different colors appear by varying rays of heat—the longest for red, the shortest for violet.

Traditions Today

Here are a few unique regional July Fourth traditions.

Seward, Alaska: The July Fourth celebration includes a six-mile footrace to the top of Mount Marathon and back.

Lititz, Pennsylvania: On the night of the Fourth, children create a Festival of Candles by lighting thousands of candles that citizens made during the winter.

Tecumseh, Nebraska: The community raises more than 200 flags around their town courthouse to remember those who have served in the country's armed forces.

⋆Talk About ⋆It   What are some of our town's Independence Day traditions?

Mormon Pioneer Day

July 24 • Mormons in the United States and worldwide

This holiday celebrates the courage and determination of the pioneer members of the Church of Jesus Christ of Latter-day Saints, known as the Mormons. It is a huge event in the state of Utah, where many Mormons live. The holiday provides a great starting point for discussing religion in American history.

Holiday History *Read Aloud*

In1847, Mormon families throughout the world found their way to the United States and began the slow and arduous journey to Salt Lake City, Utah. These were true pioneers—they abandoned their homes and set forth in wagons and on foot to cross rugged terrain, including desert, to a place where they could be among other Mormons and freely practice their religion.

For more about religions and holidays, see pages 7—9.

Traditions Today

Mormons in Utah celebrate Mormon Pioneer Day with one of the largest and oldest parades in the United States. The parade features colorful floats, bands, and clowns, and a promenade of more than 600 horses.

Krishna Janmastami

August or September • Hindus worldwide

The birthday of Krishna is an important Hindu celebration. Enjoy it by sharing some facts about the Hindu religion.

In Other Words

Janmastami means "eighth birth." Krishna is the eighth form of the god Vishnu. Hindus believe that the gods can make themselves into humans or animals to help people. Krishna's most important mission was to destroy King Kamsa, the son of a demon who brought harm to good people.

For more about Hinduism and the Hindu calendar, see page 9.

★ **Book Link**

Savitri: A Tale of Ancient India by Aaron Shepard (Albert Whitman, 1992). Picture book, all ages. Beautiful, simple version of the *Mahabharata*, India's classic tale.

★ **Teacher Resource**

Tales Alive! Ten Multicultural Folktales with Activities by Susan Milord (Williamson, 1994). All grades.

Traditions Today

On Krishna's birthday, Hindus fast for 24 hours. Throughout the day, they sing religious songs and read stories about Krishna such as the epic poem *Mahabharata*. Children stay up late to welcome the baby Krishna. Some even place his statue in a cradle to wait for him to be born, which is believed to be at midnight. When midnight comes, they break fast, and people ring bells, clang cymbals, and blow horns to celebrate. Their meal includes milk, butter, and other dairy products, which represent Krishna's favorite childhood foods.

Links in a Story Chain Social Studies

One common story type in India is the chain tale, a story where one action affects another, then another, and so on, until the final conclusion occurs only because of the first action. A famous American chain tale is "There was an old lady who swallowed a fly." Read any chain tale, and talk about why each action was important to the conclusion of the story.

National Inventors Month

August 1–31 • United States

Every student is an inventor! Celebrate the art of ingenuity while learning about interesting inventions throughout history.

★ Book Link

Toys! Amazing Stories Behind Some Great Inventions by Don Wulffson (Holt, 2000). Chapter book, intermediate. Wonderfully told stories reveal the truth behind the invention of such favorites as Legos™, Mr. Potato Head™, and video games.

★ Teacher Resource

Inventors and Inventions by Lorraine Hopping Egan (Scholastic, 1997). For grades 4–8. Creative cross-curricular activities, fascinating background information, and problem-solving investigations.

★ Web Link

Check out the Kid Zone at **http://inventorsdigest.com** for lots of links to projects for young inventors. Are well-known inventions made by people like you and me? For inspiration, check out the feature "264 Products NOT Invented by Corporations!"

Holiday History

Are all inventors old and crazy? According to a 1995 Massachusetts Institute of Technology survey, that's what people really think. So the United Inventors Association, the Academy of Applied Science, and *Inventors' Digest* invented this holiday to encourage people of all ages to be innovative and creative.

Fast Fact *Read Aloud*

It's great to play with your food! As the story goes, George Lerner's children always played with their food at the dinner table. One day, George rolled up his sleeves and played with his plate of food. He took a potato and gave it bottle caps for eyes, a strawberry on a toothpick for a nose, and a row of thumbtacks for a metallic mouth. Lerner made a toy model of his Mr. Potato Head™ and eventually sold the idea to the Hasbro company. Lerner's dinner-time play made one of the most popular toys ever!

Invention Fair `Science`

Inspire students to come up with their own ideas for useful products. Have them carefully plan their creations using simple household items, and then make them. Hold an Invention Fair so young inventors can demonstrate what they've made to fellow students, family, and friends.

Follow the Rules of Invention `Science`

Thomas Edison, the first inventor inducted into the National Inventors Hall of Fame, was awarded 1,093 U.S. patents. (A patent is a grant from the government allowing an inventor to make, use, and sell his or her invention.) As students plan and create their own inventions, make sure they follow Thomas Edison's six rules for successful inventions.

1. Don't invent useless things. (Make sure your invention is helpful!)
2. Set a goal, then stick to it.
3. List the steps for reaching your goal, then follow them.
4. Share all the data with your team of inventors.
5. Assign each team member a specific job.
6. Keep very careful records. That way, you can go back and learn from your mistakes and successes.

Name _____

Date _____

A Special Flag

Read the poem below to learn about the colors and symbols on the American flag. Color the flag.

Here's an American flag just for you.
Take out your markers: red, white, and blue.
The top box is blue, for the sky at night.
Draw 50 stars, all shiny white.
Color each stripe red, white, red, white.
For the 13 colonies and our forefathers' fight.
Remember our flag on June 14.
Enjoy what it stands for—the American dream.

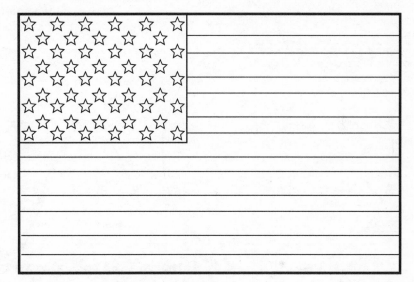

BONUS: Our forefathers chose red, white, and blue for the flag of the new United States of America. Each color has a special meaning. Write a short definition for each of the words in bold (look up the words you don't know in the dictionary). Then write why you think each symbolizes our country in its fight for independence.

★ RED ★
stands for

valor: _____

hardiness: _____

Why do you think the flag is red? _____

_____

★ WHITE ★
stands for

purity: _____

innocence: _____

Why do you think the flag is white?

_____

_____

★ BLUE ★
stands for

vigilance: _____

perseverance: _____

justice: _____

Why do you think the flag is blue?

_____

_____

Father's Day

Name _____

Date _____

Father's Day Find Out

Complete the web to tell more about your father or the special man in your life.

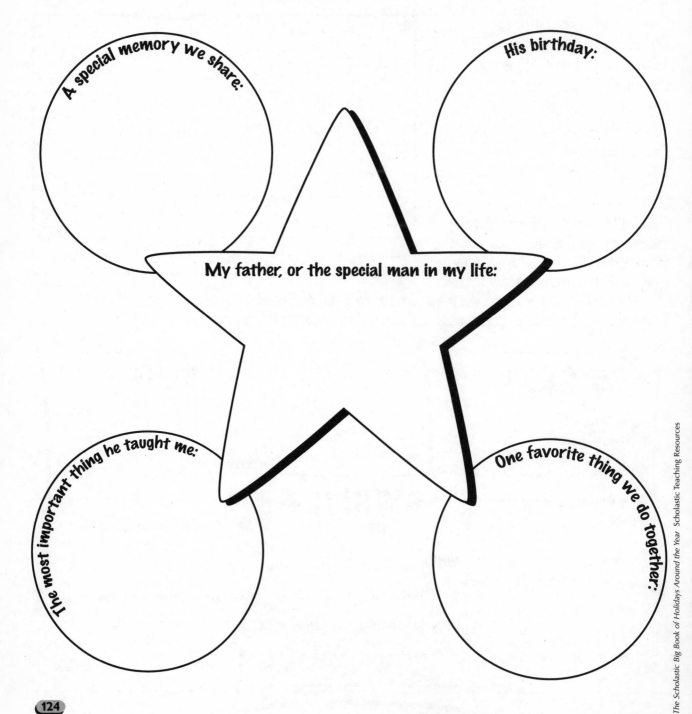

A special memory we share:

His birthday:

My father, or the special man in my life:

The most important thing he taught me:

One favorite thing we do together:

The Scholastic Big Book of Holidays Around the Year Scholastic Teaching Resources

Name _____

Independence Day

Date _____

Special Words From the Declaration of Independence

1. Give an example from your own experience of what it means to be "equal" to others?

_____

_____

We hold these truths to be self-evident,

That all men are created equal,

That they are endowed by their Creator

with certain unalienable Rights,

That among these are

Life, Liberty and the pursuit of Happiness.

—from the Declaration of Independence

2. What are some rights you have as a person who lives in the United States?

_____

_____

3. As an American, how do you enjoy liberty?

_____

_____

_____

Use one of the phrases or words from the quotation above to make an all-American bumper sticker. Create a design with the words and pictures that illustrate your meaning.

The Scholastic Big Book of Holidays Around the Year Scholastic Teaching Resources

Answers for Reproducibles

Citizenship Test, page 40

1. A. executive, legislative, judicial
2. B. executive
3. B. the 50 states and original 13 colonies
4. C. democracy
5. C. the White House
6. A. the right to vote
7. C. A and B (reading the newspaper and talking to government officials)
8. B. Philadelphia
9. B. 4 years
10. I pledge allegiance to the flag of the United States of America and to the republic for which it stands, one nation, under God, indivisible, with liberty and justice for all.

December Match Up, page 71

Hanukkah: candle, dreidel, gelt, menorah

Our Lady of Guadalupe: rose

Christmas: reindeer, star, tree

Kwanzaa: candle, kinara, mkeka

Las Posadas: candle, piñata

New Year's Eve/Day: noisemaker, resolutions

Counting on Famous Presidents, page 106

A. $1 (dollar bill); George Washington
B. $0.01 (penny); Abraham Lincoln
C. $5 (five dollar bill); Abraham Lincoln
D. $0.25 (quarter); George Washington

1. $5 + $5 + $1 +$1 = $12
2. $1 +$1 + $0.25 + $0.25 + $0.25 + $0.25 = $3
3. $5 + $5 + $5 + $0.01 + $0.01 + $0.01 + $0.01 + $0.01 + $0.01 = $15.06
4. $0.25 – ($0.01 + $0.01 + $0.01 + $0.01 + $0.01) = $0.20
5. $5 + $1 +$1 +$1 + $0.25 + $0.25 – $0.01 = $8.49

Index of Holidays